A Basketful of Taupe

Practical Projects to Decorate Your Life

by Kylie Irvine

A Basketful of Taupe
Practical projects to decorate your life

Editor: Donna di Natale
Designer: Kelly Ludwig
Photography: Aaron T. Leimkuehler
Illustration: Eric Sears
Technical Editor: Christina DeArmond
Production assistance: Jo Ann Groves

Published by:
Kansas City Star Books
1729 Grand Blvd.
Kansas City, Missouri, USA 64108
All rights reserved

First edition, first printing
ISBN: 978-1-61169-082-8
Library of Congress Control Number: 2001012345
Printed in the United States of America by Walsworth
Publishing Co., Marceline, MO
To order copies, call StarInfo at (816) 234-4242 and say
"Books."

www.PickleDish.com

Table of Contents

About the Author..2

Acknowledgements 3

Introduction 4

General Instructions 5

Resources 13

Projects

    Basket Quilt..14

    Basket Pillow Cover and Wall Hanging 32

    Taupe About Town Bag 35

    Petal Basket Bag..38

    Tumbling Block Pincushion 41

    Petal Pin Cushion 43

    Basket Needle Case 44

    Basket Notebook Cover 47

    Sewing Case...51

    Triangle Pincushion 54

    Project or Pattern Binder Cover.......................56

Templates...60

    Block 1 and 13.. 61

    Block 2..62

    Block 3..63

    Block 4 64

    Block 5..65

    Block 6 and 8...66

    Block 7..67

    Block 9 68

    Block 10 69

    Block 11 70

    Block 12 71

    Basket A Piecing 72

    Basket A Handle..73

    Basket A 74

    Basket B 75

    Basket C 76

    Basket D 77

    Basket E 78

    Basket F 79

    Basket G 80

    Basket H 81

    Piecing for Basket I...82

    Basket I 83

    Basket J 84

    Basket K 85

    Basket L 86

    Taupe About Town Bag Back Piecing 87

    Taupe About Town Bag Front Piecing 88

    Flower Outline for Taupe About Town Bag....................90

    Petal Bag and Pincushion Templates.............89

    Petal Pincushion Diagram...............................89

    Needle Case Appliqué....................................90

    Notebook Cover Appliqué............................... 91

    Sewing Case Appliqué and Embroidery 92

    Tumbling Block Templates 93

    Project Binder Appliqué and Words 94

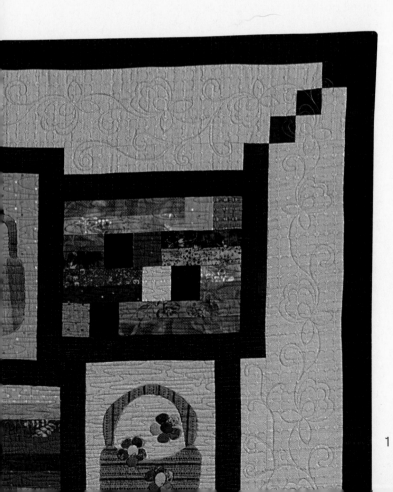

About the Author

I have loved fabric and color for as long as I can remember. My mum often reminds me that as soon as I was old enough to use scissors, I was cutting up colored paper into little pieces and sticking them into patterns. Throughout my childhood, I continued to love sewing and everything creative. I even took oil painting and folk art classes, and learned to crochet and embroider when I was just a young girl.

During my final year of university, I took a patchwork class at a local store. After making Log Cabin, Churn Dash and Star pattern cushions, I was enthralled. After university I was lucky to receive an internship at the Chicago Apparel Center. While there I visited the Smithsonian museum in Washington, D.C., to see the Antique Quilts and was truly inspired by the patchwork.

On returning to New Zealand, I started my working career in textiles and marketing and took up patchwork as a serious hobby, taking a class each week for several years.

It wasn't for another eight years, in 2002, that I made the huge leap to leave my marketing career to start my own patchwork business where I specialize in pretty floral and Taupe fabrics. I started designing patterns using Taupe fabrics that I imported directly from Japan because they weren't available in England at the time. My naïve little flower designs were an instant success with my customers and so it was the focus of my first book, **Taupe Inspirations.** I love flowers so much that, of course, I had to include some in this latest book with my basket designs.

Although born and raised in New Zealand, I have lived in Australia, America and Sweden, and now live just outside of London, in Buckinghamshire, England, with my husband, Murray, my two wonderful daughters, Emily and Maisie, and a super soppy golden retriever called Lucy.

Kylie

Kylie@kylieirvine.com
Ph: +4477-65888-136
www.kylieirvine.com

Acknowledgements

This book would not have come together so easily without the wonderful fabrics and products available today — and of course the help and support I have received along the way from some very special people.

Special thanks must go to my daughters (now 2 ½ and 6 ½) and my husband who have become very used to me sewing and typing patterns into the night. They have been very supportive along the way and love the creative results, as one project sparks another.

A huge thank you to Nireko and Lecien USA for all the beautiful Lecien fabrics used in this book. The Cosmo embroidery thread really lends itself to be used with the Taupe fabrics, and it is so wonderful to work with. The projects really were a dream to design and stitch.

Thank you to Rachel from Creative Grids Rulers for the fabulous rulers. They are a breeze to use and result in perfect shapes. There were so many I wanted to use, it was hard to pick just a couple as my favorites.

A final huge thank you to Kansas City Star Quilts. You are a wonderful and talented team of people. Special thanks must go to Doug Weaver and Diane McLendon for setting me off on another book journey and to Donna di Natale — it has been a pleasure to work with you again as editor. Of course Aaron's photos and Kelly's designs truly make the book special and a joy for the reader.

Introduction

Somewhere in my life I became a basket collector. I never intended it to happen, but I have them in almost every room of my house and my workroom, and there seems to be an increasing collection in my loft as they get rotated through the house for seasonal displays or special events. Fortunately, baskets are just so useful for decorating, storing toys and sewing things, displaying cookies and baking, or my favorite — stuffing them full of my latest collection of 'must have' fabric. So this book is my collection of 'fabric' baskets made from my favorite Japanese Taupes. I hope you enjoy adding them to your collection, too.

Each basket in the large quilt is slightly different. I have used a variety of techniques, bias strips, traditional appliqué, pieced fabrics that are then appliquéd, and a tiny bit of foundation piecing. The different techniques make the quilt more interesting to make, but you may choose to make all the baskets alike, or just pick a few of your favorites to use on the quilt or pillow covers. All of the baskets are achievable by all levels of quilter.

When I was writing this book, both of my daughters loved to watch me make the projects. They are both obsessed with handbags and it is a wonder that the Taupe About Town bag (page 35) or the Petal Bag (page 38) made it into the box to be shipped off for photography. The bags kept disappearing on their little arms. I love the Petal Bag, as it is great for stashing your sewing things in and also makes a fabulous gift bag that is relatively simple and quick to complete.

As with all things practical, I want them to look pretty too. A simple box would do to keep your sewing things in, but it's so much fun to make the sewing case cover (page 51) and triangle pincushion (page 54) and even more fun to use them. These sewing cases are designed in Japan, so they go perfectly with the Taupe fabrics and Cosmo Embroidery threads that I love.

I hope you have as much fun making the projects as I had designing them for you.

Happy Sewing

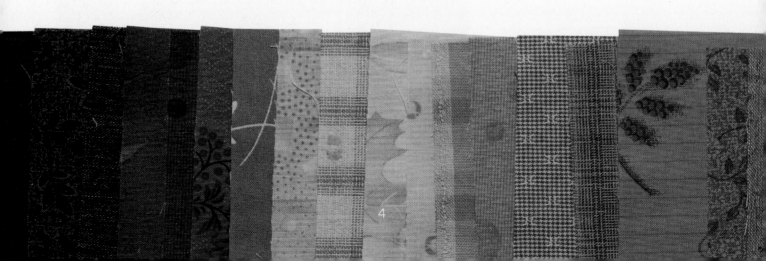

General Instructions

Fabric Selection

Selecting just which fabric to use can be such an enjoyable part of quiltmaking. I try to make the decision over several days. I start with absolutely everything I think might work from my stash and from fabrics I have purchased. Over a few days, I take out anything that doesn't work and make a list of the fabrics I absolutely need. To help with 'jurying' my fabric, I arrange them in color groups and blend them from one color to the next. Every few days, I check back and make changes until I have the perfect group of fabrics for my project. I always start with more fabrics than I need, as it is much easier to take out fabrics than add in new fabrics later.

Just like with other fabrics, when using Taupe fabrics you need to have light, medium and dark tones and a variety of prints. Quilts and projects are so much more interesting to look at if you use a wide variety of both prints and wovens, such as small prints, large florals, geometrics, plaids and stripes, dots and anything with a lovely texture. Many fabric mills run basic collections to complement the fashion Taupe collections and these are often smaller, simpler prints. I like to have lots of these basics in my stash as they can slip into so many projects to complement bolder patterns and designs. Remember to look at fabrics you don't instantly fall in love with, as sometimes a little piece

of these in your quilts can add zing. I am not instantly drawn to blue, but all my quilts have a shade or two of blue or blue/grey somewhere, as it complements the other colors I use.

Fabric Yardage

If you are using a large print fabric, you can cut it in several different places so that it looks like you have used several different fabrics when you have only used the one.

If I have stated an equivalent amount of fabric in the supplies list, for example 3 yards for appliqué and pieced blocks, this means you can use various sizes of fabrics to make up the full amount of 3 yards. This could be fat eighths, a scrap bag of bits from your stash or quilt store, a roll of strips, charm packs, fat quarters or any other size you can think of, and you can use as many or as few fabrics as you like.

Seam Allowances

You will need to add a ¼" to all of the appliqué templates, as the line shown is the seam line. The pieced blocks have a ¼" seam allowance included in the measurements.

Pinning

When you are sewing prints and wovens together, it is good practice to pin your fabrics so that they don't slip when you are stitching them. I like to piece with my walking foot on my machine; this stops any of the unruly woven textures from moving as they pass between the foot of the machine and the feed dogs and means I can get away with pinning less.

Pressing

Press all your seams to one side, toward the darkest fabric, and make your block as flat as possible. There are some exceptions to this — please watch out for these in the instructions. In some individual blocks in the large quilt, I have recommended pressing in different directions as this will give the block a different look, especially the window and spool type blocks.

Stitching Guide

Before beginning a project with embroidery, trace or draw the embroidery lines onto your fabric. I like to embroider without a hoop, using a very light fusible behind the fabric. This helps to hide your threads and stabilizes your fabric so it is easier to sew. I have used Cosmo embroidery thread for all the embroidery in this book. Cosmo is a Japanese thread that is becoming widely available in most countries. I really like the Cosmo Multiwork 322 thread; it comes on a roll, and is ready to use as a 2-stranded embroidery thread. Unlike the 6-stranded thread in a skein, there is no need to separate the individual threads; it's ready to go right off the roll. If you are like me and don't know what to do with those leftover strands, then you will love this thread, too. Cosmo thread blends beautifully with the Taupe fabrics.

Cosmo thread used for embroidery:

▷ Note Book Cover: 233, 235 and 368

▷ Project Folder: 235

▷ Needle Case: 235, 368, 652 and 369

▷ Sewing Case: 236

▷ Taupe About Town Bag: 467 and 923

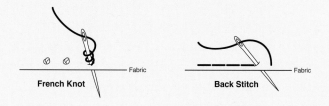

French Knot — Fabric   **Back Stitch** — Fabric

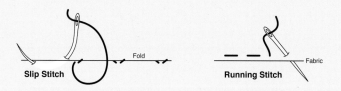

Slip Stitch — Fold   **Running Stitch** — Fabric

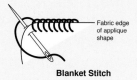

Fabric edge of applique shape

Blanket Stitch

Rulers

There is a vast array of rulers available and, in the past, I was one of those people who had one longer ruler, a square one and a couple of in-between sizes. Most of the other rulers just seemed like gadgets. But of late I have been using some of the wonderful rulers that allow you to cut 'template' pieces from strips, and they truly do give you perfect pieces for sewing together. I am really taken with the Tumbler Block ruler from Creative Grids, the one I used for the back of the binder cover on page 56 and also for the basket on the notebook cover on page 47.

To use this type of ruler, cut the size strip as indicated on the ruler, in this case it is 4 ½", and then place the ruler on the fabric strip.

Cut up and down each side of the tumbler shape, and you will get perfect tumbler pieces quickly and without any waste. Every second piece is automatically cut upside down, just like you piece them together. Once you are proficient with the ruler, you can layer several strips at a time so that you are cutting several colors of tumbler pieces in one go.

The 60-degree equilateral triangle ruler works in the same way, and I used this ruler to make the pieces for the pocket of the Sewing Case on page 51. I also use this ruler to cut smaller size pieces. Just cut your strip narrower and move the ruler along to align the raw edges with the ruler after each piece is cut from the strip.

The rectangular ruler that is perfect for my pieced

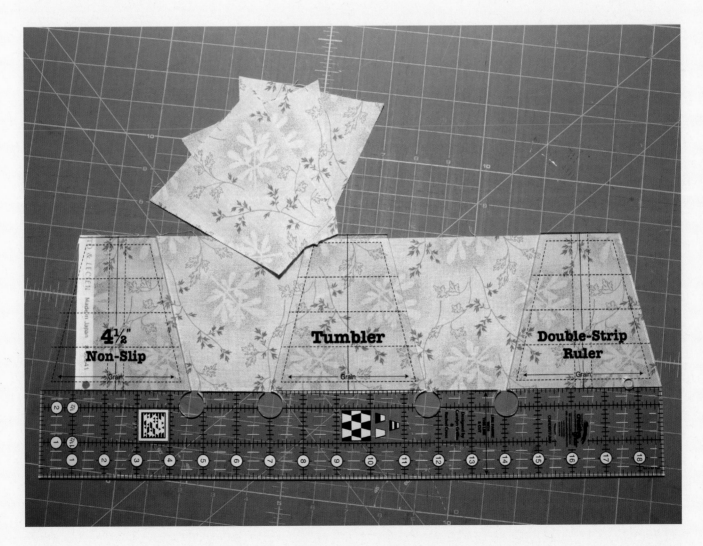

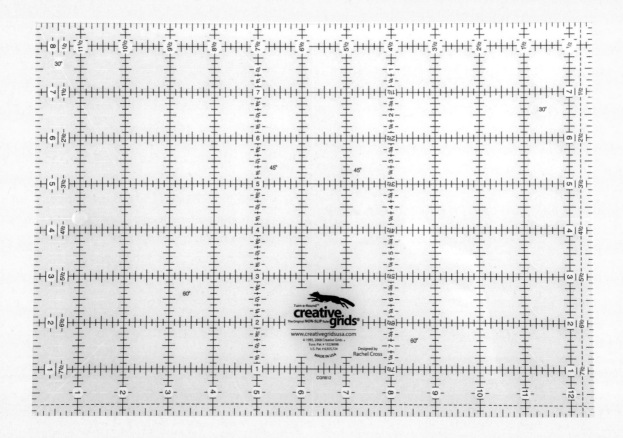

blocks is the 8 ½" x 12 ½" ruler, also by Creative Grids. The blocks in the large basket quilt are all trimmed to 8 ½" by 11 ½" before stitching the sashing, and this ruler makes it really easy to trim and square up accurately. The best bit about these three rulers is that they all have gripper spots on the underside, so they won't move while you are cutting. This makes them safer to use and more accurate, too.

Trims, Embellishments

I love buying embellishments, and I love some of the pieces so much I don't want to use them until I have just the right project. One of my favorite antique buttons and a piece of a favorite velvet ribbon are used on the Petal pincushion. I designed the pincushion fabric around the button and ribbon, so sometimes its good to start with your embellishment and then choose your fabric to match.

On the needle case, I used the sew-on type magnetic snaps, as you can put them in just the right spot once you have finished making the needle case. These items should all be available from your local quilt store.

Freezer Paper Appliqué

I like to use the freezer paper method to appliqué, so I have included instructions for this method here. You may fuse the appliqué and blanket stitch it, or use the needle-turn method of appliqué, whichever technique you prefer. However, if you are going to fuse the appliqué, you will have to **reverse** the appliqué patterns as these are drawn for freezer paper or needle-turn appliqué.

Trace each pattern piece onto the dull side of the freezer paper, leaving enough space between each piece to cut them out. You can mark areas that will tuck under other pieces with a dashed line. Cut these pieces out on the drawn line.

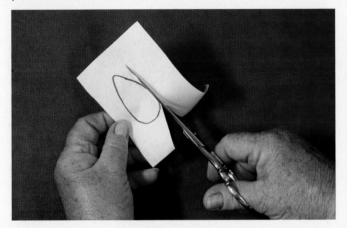

Position the freezer paper pattern piece shiny side down onto the <u>right</u> side of your appliqué fabric. Press in place gently with a warm iron (no steam is recommended). Do not slide your iron, as this could move the freezer paper.

Trim your fabric around the freezer paper leaving a ¼" seam allowance and, as much as possible, on the edges which will tuck under other fabric pieces. You can trim this off later if necessary.

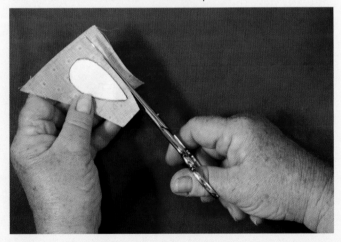

Now peel the freezer paper away from the fabric, and place it dull side down on the <u>wrong</u> side of your fabric (the shiny side will be face up). Make sure you have the freezer paper aligned so you have ¼" seam allowance around all sides of the freezer paper.

With a warm iron press the seam allowance over onto the shiny side of the freezer paper. Start by folding in any seam allowance at points and then working around the curves. Where you have a dashed line you do not need to press the seam allowance over as this area will be tucked under another piece.

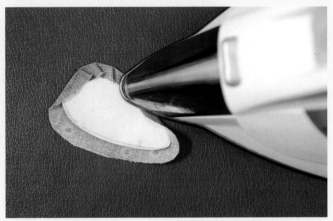

If you have a light box, lightly trace the layout guide onto your background fabric using a pencil or pen that will wash out or disappear when dampened. If you do not have a light box, you can tape your pattern sheet and the background fabric to a window to trace the layout guide onto the fabric.

Pin, tack or glue baste the appliqué pieces on the marked background fabric, making sure the pieces are tucked under one another in the correct order (the dashed lines on the pattern piece should be tucked under the adjacent pattern pieces).

Starting with the lowest piece (the one that tucks under the other pieces the most) stitch the pieces in place. I like to use a blind stitch so my stitches are not seen, but you could blanket stitch with a coordinating thread or any other stitch you prefer. If you machine appliqué using a buttonhole stitch, I recommend you use a smoke-colored transparent thread for Taupe. If you use a running stitch or blind stitch I recommend using a matching cotton thread. I like to use a dark Taupe color or a soft grey, whichever blends the best.

Remove the freezer paper from your appliqué by carefully cutting a small hole or slit in the background fabric behind each appliqué piece (a pair of tweezers is very helpful for removing the freezer paper). If you are making the large quilt, I recommend leaving the freezer paper in until you have the whole quilt stitched together because it helps keep the appliqué in shape (you just have to remember to remove the freezer paper before you baste the quilt for quilting). If you like your appliqué to puff up more when you quilt, you can trim the background fabric away ¼" inside the stitching line of each appliqué piece. Just be careful to not cut into the appliqué piece.

Easy Mitered Corners

A mitered corner is one where two pieces of fabric join at a 45-degree angle rather than the normal 90-degree angle you see on straight pieced blocks. Many quilters shy away from mitered corners but they are actually quite simple, and I hope that by following these few steps, you will find making mitered corner blocks is easy and enjoyable.

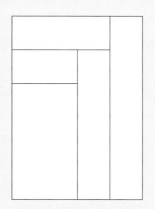

Straight Pieced Block

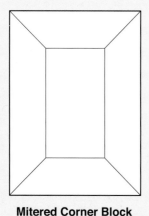

Mitered Corner Block

Begin by finding the middle of each piece you are going to stitch so that you can align the pieces at the center, leaving an even amount at each end. Mark ¼" in from each edge of the center rectangle with a pin. Stitch between these marks using a ¼" seam allowance. I recommend you backstitch or use a locking stitch at the start and stop points, as you do not want your stitches to come undone.

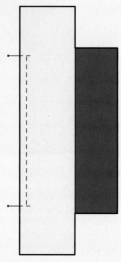

Fold one end of the long strip down (wrong sides together) so that it is away from the seam allowance. You may pin this to keep it away from where you will stitch next.

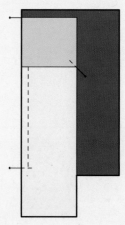

Having found the middle of the next side piece, pin this in place, mark the points where you will stop, and start sewing ¼" in from each edge of the center rectangle. Stitch between the pins.

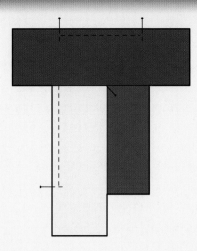

Repeat these steps until you have all four sides and corners completed. Press gently with an iron.

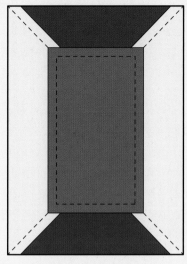

Matching the narrow edges of the two side pieces and with right sides together, pin the two pieces together and mark a 45 degree line from the ¼" point to the outside corner. Check to make sure your center rectangle is not in the way of the line you have drawn. Stitch along this line starting at the ¼" point and sewing right to the corner.

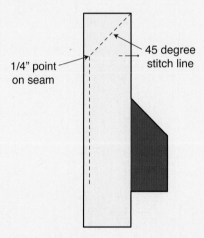

1/4" point on seam

45 degree stitch line

Traditionally, mitered corners are pressed open. However, I like the seams pressed to one side so that the block has more of a 3-dimensional look. This is especially important when you are making the spool blocks, where the top, bottom and center fabrics are similar in shade. You want these pieces to stand out so the seams should be pressed toward these fabrics. On window/standard type blocks, press your seams away from the center. With all pressing, please consider that your block should be as flat as possible, so if it is better to press your seams open or in the other direction, feel free to do so. Trim the excess seam allowance on the mitered corner to ¼".

Open the stitched pieces out and press gently with your fingers.

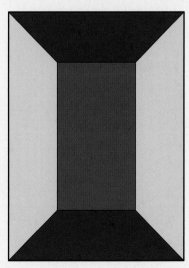

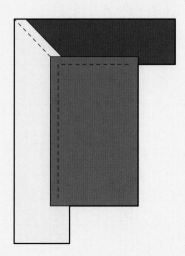

Measurements for Blocks, Sashing and Borders

The measurements given for sashing, borders and binding assume that your blocks measure the same as the sizes listed in the pattern. Before cutting your sashing, check that your blocks measure the same as the instructions in the book. The same for your quilt top — measure before you cut. If your measurements are different from those in the instructions, adjust the measurements to fit your quilt. If your blocks are smaller than the measurement given in the book, I recommend you trim all your blocks to measure the same size as the smallest block.

Quilting

I love the look of hand quilting but just don't have the time, so many of my projects are now machine quilted. I use a long arm quilter to quilt my large quilts and machine quilt the smaller projects myself. If you are using a long arm quilter, check to make sure that they have quilted textured fabrics before (if you have used them in your quilt). They will need to adjust the sensitivity of their machine so it does not view the textures as obstructions.

The quilting on the large basket quilt was completed on a long arm machine and was stitched in the ditch around each basket, and then all the blocks and sashing were filled with a water pattern. The border has a lovely floral vine with swirly tendrils to fill up the spaces around the flowers.

Resources

I have used a wide variety of fabrics in the projects, so I've listed the companies below that supply or distribute these products. Most items are widely available, and you can check the websites for a store near you that stocks these products. If you have difficulty finding any of the products locally, please visit my website, www.kylieirvine.com, as we carry these products.

Taupe Fabric and Cosmo Thread

Lecien U.S.A., Inc.
5515 Doyle Street, Suite 6
Emeryville, Calif. 94608
Ph 510 596 3085
www.lecienusa.com
Lecien Corporation Art/Hobby Division
Yotsubashi Grand Square1-28-3
ShinmachiNishi-ku,
Osaka 550-0013
Japan
81-6-4390-5516
www.lecien.co.jp/en/hobby/

Taupe Fabrics

Daiwabo Co., Ltd
Midosujidaiwa Bldg.,
6-8Kyutaromachi 3-Chome,
Chuo-KuOsaka, 541-0056
Japan
81 6 6281 2428
sales@daiwabo.net
U.S.A. Distributor
Pinwheels Trading Corp
2006 Albany Post Road
Croton-on-Hudson, NY 10520
888 346 0711
www.pinwheelstrading.com

Patterns and Sewing Cases

Kylie Irvine at Antique Angel Patchwork
kylie@antiqueangel.co.uk
004477-65888-136
www.kylieirvine.com or www.antiqueangel.co.uk

Creative Grids Rulers

Creative Grids USA
400 W. Dussel Dr.
Maumee, Ohio 43537
www.creativegridsusa.com
Creative Grids (UK) Limited
23A Pate Road
Melton Mowbray, Leicestershire,
LE13 0RG
England
0044 1664 501724
www.creativegrids.com

Wool Fabric

Weeks Dye Works, Inc
1510-103 Mechanical Blvd.
Garder, N.C. 27529
1-877-OVERDYE (1-877-683-7393)
www.weeksdyeworks.com

Basket Quilt

FINISHED SIZE: 71" SQUARE
BLOCK SIZE: 8" X 11" FINISHED

Fabric and Supplies

This quilt can be made with as few or as many fabrics as you like. I like to use lots of different fabrics with a mix of prints and woven textures. Texture adds interest and gives a softer look to the quilt. You will need the equivalent of at least 6 ½ yards for the pieced blocks and appliquéd flowers. Charm packs and/or fat eighths are excellent to get you started, and you may want to purchase fat quarters of the fabrics you really love. You can also use scraps and fabric from your stash and add fabrics as you go along. As many of the handles for the baskets are made from bias strips, I recommend you purchase a fat quarter of the fabrics you plan to use for baskets, as this will ensure you have enough for the length of the handle without piecing it.

- ▷ 6 ½ yards (or equivalent) for the appliqué pieces and pieced blocks
- ▷ 12 – 9" x 12" pieces for the appliqué block background
- ▷ 1 ¼ yards for the sashing
- ▷ 1 ½ yards for the inner border
- ▷ ⅝ yard for the outer border
- ▷ ½ yard for the binding if using woven (textured) fabric; ¾ yard (if using a printed fabric for binding)
- ▷ 5 ½ yards for the backing
- ▷ Batting: Full Size (84" x 100")

Because the blocks and sashing for this quilt are not cut or stitched in the traditional way, you should read all of the instructions before you begin and study the photograph on page 27. I recommend that you complete your quilt in 4 steps: 1) appliqué blocks; 2) pieced blocks; 3) sashing and borders; 4) putting it all together. I also recommend that you cut fabrics when you are ready for each step so you can check the sizes required as you work through the quilt.

Basket Blocks

FINISHED SIZE: 8" WIDE BY 11" TALL
TEMPLATES ARE ON PAGES 72-85

The Baskets B, C, I and K are cut from constructed pieces of fabric. Refer to the templates for how to construct the fabric pieces, and then cut the basket shapes. For all the appliquéd basket blocks, center the appliqué in the middle of the background fabric, and then trim to 8 ½" x 11 ½" after you have completed the appliqué.

Tip: Label each basket block as you complete it. This will make assembling the quilt easier.

Basket A - Basket

For a quickie method, work from the front starting with the bottom left piece. Lay your fabric for this piece on the template, lining up the bottom of your fabric with the bottom line on the pattern. The fabric should overlap the stitch line by about ¼". Lay the next piece of fabric face down on top of the first piece, keeping the top edges even. Sew on Stitch Line 1. Flip piece 2 open and press.

Take the third piece and lay it face down on the second piece, and place it so that it is slightly offset as shown in the diagram. Repeat this method until you have all seven pieces stitched down. Remove the paper gently, and you are ready to cut your appliqué handle for the arch.

Baskets B, E, F and L

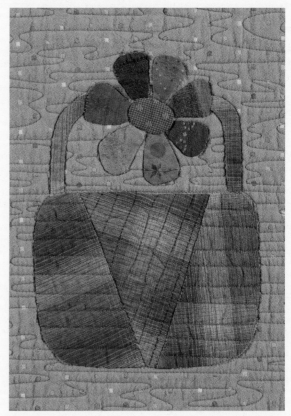

To construct Basket A, cut the pieces according to the measurements in the piecing diagram on page 72. Join the pieces together into columns and then stitch each column to the next. Press the seams to one side as you go. Use this rectangle to cut the basket appliqué on page 74.

Basket A - Handle

The fabric for this handle is foundation pieced. If you are experienced, you can stitch the pieces together by aligning them with the guide and you won't need to sew them to the paper guide on page 73. Otherwise, follow these directions for Foundation Piecing to make the pieced fabric for the basket handle.

Photocopy the pattern on page 73. If you are using the traditional foundation piecing method, work from the back of the paper pattern and stitch on the dashed lines in the order shown. Note that you will have lots of raw edges, but the aim is to make an arch from which you can cut your basket handle.

The baskets, handles and flowers for these blocks can be appliquéd using your favorite method. It is easiest to pin and appliqué the basket first, the handle next, and then the flowers.

The handles and latticework on these baskets are made using bias strips. First cut 1" wide bias strips from your chosen fat quarters. Take each bias strip and fold in one raw edge along the long side about ¼" to ⅓" and press. Repeat on the other long side, so that the bias is about ⅓ its original width and no raw edges are showing.

Cut the basket fabric according to the templates. Lay the lattice pieces over your basket fabric, as shown in the diagrams, and pin in place. Weave the strips over and under. The ends will tuck under the basket when it is appliquéd to the background.

Refer to the templates for placing the baskets and handles on the background fabric. Pin and appliqué.

Baskets G

Basket I

▷ Cut 4 – 1 ¾" x 2" pieces. Sew them together along the 2" sides.

▷ Cut 2 – 3 ½" x 5" pieces. Sew a piece to each side of the center squares.

Use this constructed piece to cut the basket appliqué on page 80.

The handle is made from a 1" x 14" bias strip. Take the bias strip and fold in one raw edge along the long side about ¼" to ⅓" and press. Repeat on the other long side, so that the bias is about ⅓ its original width and no raw edges are showing.

Refer to the template for placing the basket and handle on the background fabric. Pin and appliqué.

To make the basket, you will need to cut 8 pieces of fabric for the strips. I used one directional fabric cut two different directions. You can do this or you can use two similar fabrics to achieve the same effect. Cut the strips according to the template on page 82.

If you are using one fabric, cut 4 strips in a vertical direction and 4 in a horizontal direction. If you are using two different fabrics, they can all be cut in one direction from each fabric.

Make the fabric rectangle by piecing the strips into rows and then sew the rows together. Cut the appliqué shape from this rectangle.

Refer to the template on page 83 for placing the basket and handle on the background fabric. Pin and appliqué.

Basket C, G, J and K Handles

Cut 4 – 1 ¾" x 2" pieces. Sew them together. To make the bias handles for these baskets, cut 1" bias strips from your chosen fabrics. Take each bias strip and fold in one raw edge along the long side about ¼" to ⅓" and press. Repeat on the other long side, so that the bias is about ⅓ its original width and no raw edges are showing. Press each handle strip into a rough curve with your iron. This makes it easier to position the handles on your appliqué background.

Refer to the templates for placing the baskets and handles on the background fabric. Pin and appliqué.

Pieced Blocks

FINISHED BLOCK SIZE: 11" WIDE X 8" TALL

TEMPLATES ON PAGES 61-71

When you are cutting the fabrics for the pieced blocks, it is a good idea to label each piece with the block number and the fabric number or its location so you can identify it on the layout diagram provided for each block. I like to use sticky labels and label A, B, C for each row and then number the pieces in each row from left to right, 1, 2, 3, etc., so that the top left piece is A1 and so on. If you do get a piece in the wrong place according to the layout diagram, don't unpick. Just call it a design feature, as the pieced blocks are scrappy and it will still look great.

Tip: When each block is completed, label it with the block number. This will make assembling the quilt much easier.

Block 1

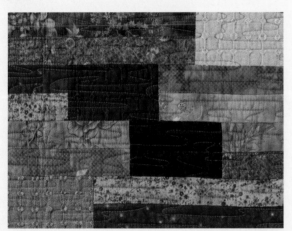

Follow the diagram on page 61 for constructing Block 1.

This block is made up of 4 row sets. Each row has 2 or 4 narrow strips and one larger rectangle.

First sew the narrow pieces for this block into sets, then stitch them to the sides of the larger rectangles. Repeat for the other three row sets, and then sew the rows together.

Block 2

Follow the diagram on page 62 for constructing Block 2.

Sew 4 strips together. Make 4 sets. Sew a vertical strip to one side of each set. Sew 2 sets together to make a row, and then sew the 2 rows together.

Block 3

This block is made up of 4 rows; each row has 2 or 4 narrow strips and 2 large rectangles. Following the diagram on page 63 for constructing Block 3.

First sew the narrow pieces into sets of 2, and then stitch them to the sides of the larger rectangles. Join the 2 larger rectangles together along the 2 ½" sides to make a row. Repeat for the other 3 rows, and then sew the rows together.

Block 4

Follow the diagram on page 64 for constructing this block.

First sew the pieces together along the 1 ½" side so that you have 8 strips, each measuring approximately 11 ½" long. Sew each strip to the next one until you have all 8 strips sewn together.

Block 5

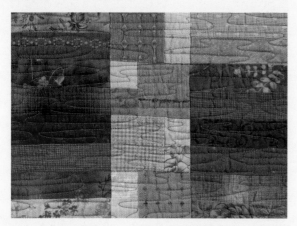

This block is made up of three sections: a left hand column of strips, a right hand column of strips, and a center column made up of smaller and larger squares. Follow the diagram on page 65 for constructing Block 5.

First stitch the center section by sewing 2 small squares together, and then sewing this rectangle to the large square. Repeat for the other small and large squares. Sew all 4 of these together following the layout diagram. Next stitch your columns of strips together, and then sew these to each side of the center column.

Block 6

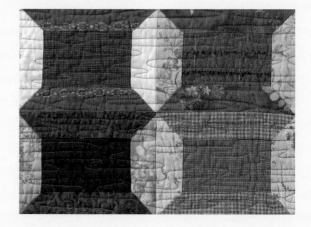

Follow the diagram on page 66 to construct Block 6.

This spool block is easy to piece following the easy mitered corner instructions on page 10. Make each spool first and then sew them together following the layout diagram. Make sure the top and bottom strips around the center rectangle are a similar or a darker color than the center rectangle to ensure that you get the spool effect.

Block 7

Follow the diagram on page 67 to construct Block 7.

First sew the pieces for this block together along the long side to make 4 sets of 4 or 5 strips. Then sew the top left set of 5 strips to the top right set of 4 strips. Repeat for the lower 2 sets of strips. Sew these together to make the block.

Block 8

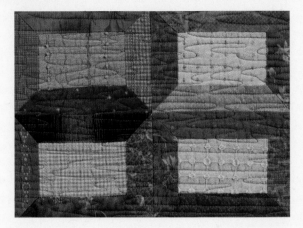

Follow the diagram on page 66 to construct Block 8.

This window block is easy to piece following the easy mitered corner instructions on page 10. To ensure that you end up with windows (not spools), make sure the center rectangle is lighter than the four strips surrounding it. Sew the windows together following the layout diagram.

Block 9

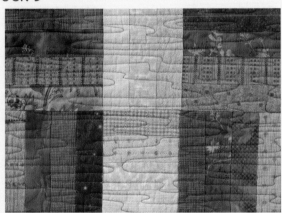

Follow the diagram on page 68 to construct Block 9.

This block is made up of 6 sections of strips. Sew the long sides of the strip sets together, and then sew the 3 top sections to each other following the layout diagram. Repeat for the lower sets of strips. Sew the top and bottom sections together to complete this block.

Block 10

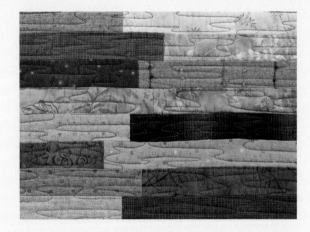

Follow the diagram on page 69 to construct Block 10.

Sew the pieces for this block together along the 1 ½" seams first so you have 8 strips measuring approximately 11 ½" long. Then stitch each strip to the next one until you have all 8 strips sewn together according to the block diagram.

Block 11

Follow the diagram on page 70 to construct Block 11.

This block is made up of 4 rows; each row has 2 or 4 narrow strips and 2 squares. First sew the long narrow pieces into sets of 2 and squares into sets of 2 each. Then sew the sets together according to the diagram to form rows. Sew the rows together to make the block.

Block 12

Follow the diagram on page 71 to construct Block 12.

This looks like a tricky block but is relatively simple. It is made up of three columns as indicated on the diagram.

Begin by making a log cabin block. Start with square A. Sew piece B to one side of A. Then attach piece C and then D. Sew 3 – 1 ½" x 4 ½" strips together. Sew this section to one side of the log cabin block, and 1 – 1 ½ x 4 ½" strip to the opposite side. This completes Column 1.

For the second column, make a log cabin block in the same manner as for Column 1. Sew 4 – 1 ½" x 4 ½" strips together. Sew this section perpendicular to the log cabin section (see diagram).

For the third column, begin by making a log cabin block, but leave off the final piece (use 1 square and only 3 strips). Sew 3 – 1 ½ x 4 ½" squares together, and then sew this section to the partial log cabin block.

To complete the block, sew the columns together to create the block.

Block 13

Follow the diagram on page 61 to construct Block 13.

This block is made up of 4 row sets; each row has 2 or 4 narrow strips and 1 rectangle. Sew the narrow pieces into sets of 2 first, and then stitch them to the sides of the rectangle. Repeat for the other 3 row sets, and then sew the rows together to complete the block.

Sashing and Borders

Please read all instructions for sashing before you cut anything, as this quilt is not made in the traditional manner.

Cutting Instructions

From your sashing fabric cut:
  ▷ 60 – 2" x 11 ½" rectangles
  ▷ 16 – 2" squares (set aside and label 12 of these for the corner squares on the inner border)

I used directional fabric in my quilt because it gives it so much more interest and movement. Therefore, these instructions are written for directional fabric, although you can use non-directional fabric if you wish.

You will need to cut 30 strips in each direction, i.e., 30 cut vertically on the fabric and 30 cut horizontally on the fabric. I have included a diagram to show you exactly how to cut your sashing fabric if it is directional.

Cutting Directional Fabric

Make sure the cut edges of your fabric are straight.

▷ Cut 1 – 11 ½" x the full width of the fabric (WOF) piece. Remove the selvage edges and then sub cut into 21 – 2" x 11 ½" horizontal strips.

▷ Next cut 1 – 13" x WOF piece. Remove the selvage edges, and then sub cut this vertically into two sections: 1 – 13" x 18" and 1 – 13" x 24". Now cut the 13" x 18" piece into 9 – 2" x 13" horizontal strips. Cut the 13" x 24" piece into 6 – 2" x 24" vertical strips. Sub cut these strips into 2" x 11 ½" strips.

▷ Cut the remaining fabric into 6 – 2" x WOF vertical strips. Sub cut each strip into 2" x 11 ½" vertical strips.

You should end up with 30 horizontal strips and 30 vertical strips, each 2" x 11 ½". I recommend you place these in bags marked "vertical" and "horizontal."

Using the diagram below, trim the left hand edge of the fabric from selvage to selvage so it is straight. Mark a point at 11 ½" along the selvage. Cut along this line and then sub cut the rectangle into 21 – 2" x 11 ½" strips (these are horizontal cuts).

Next mark the point 13" along, and cut 9 horizontal strips from the top. These will need to be trimmed to 11 ½" once cut. From this remaining section cut 6 vertical strips 2" x 24". Sub cut each strip into two 11 ½" long pieces. Finally, from the remaining fabric cut 6 – 2" wide vertical strips; sub cut each of these strips into three 11 ½" long pieces and three 2" squares.

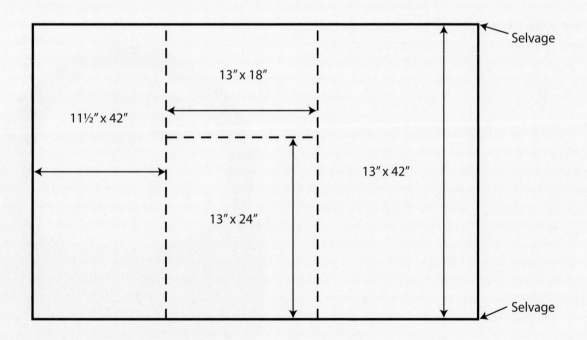

25

Cutting Non Directional Fabric

If you do not have a directional fabric (or are not concerned that your directional fabric will run in two directions) cut 20 strips 2" wide by the full width of fabric (approximately 42"). Sub-cut 8 of the strips into 3 – 2" x 11 ½" strips plus 2 – 2" squares. From the remaining 12 strips, cut 3 – 2" x 11 ½" strips.

Inner Border

From the Inner Border fabric cut 8 – 5" x WOF strips. Trim the selvage from the end of each strip and square the end up if necessary. Set these aside.

Next cut 4 – 2" x WOF strips. Sub cut 3 strips into 3 – 2" x 11 ½" pieces and 2 – 2" x 3 ½" pieces. From the 4th strip cut 1 – 2" x 11 ½" strip, 6 – 2" x 3 ½" pieces, and 8 – 2" x 2" squares.

Outer Border

From the Outer Border fabric cut 8 – 2" x WOF strips. Trim the selvage from the end of each strip and square the end up if necessary. Please check that your quilt measures 67 ½ " square. If it measures smaller or larger than this you will need to adjust the border measurements to fit your quilt. If you are not using directional fabrics, sew the sashing to the blocks but still make sure your blocks are going in the right direction.

Binding

If you are using a textured woven fabric for your binding, cut 8 – 1 ¾" x WOF strips for a single binding.

If you are using a non-textured printed fabric, cut your binding strips 2 ½" x WOF. Trim off the selvage edges and square up the ends if necessary. Label these pieces Binding and set aside.

Assembling the quilt

Press and measure all 25 blocks. The basket blocks should measure 8 ½" wide by 11 ½" tall. The pieced blocks should measure 11 ½" wide by 8 ½" tall. If your blocks are larger, trim to this size. If you have blocks that are smaller, I recommend you trim all of the blocks to match the smallest size block you have made and adjust the sashing measurements below to fit your blocks. All seams are ¼" and pressed to one side as directed in each step.

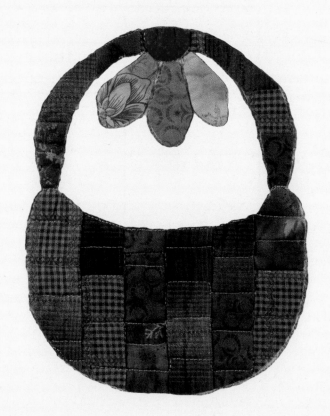

Sashing

The instructions here are given for directional fabric that has been cut horizontally and vertically. Please refer to the quilt layout diagram to check which way the blocks will lay before you sew to make sure that all the fabrics are running in the same direction.

▷ Sew one horizontally cut sashing piece (2" x 11 ½") to each long side of the basket blocks.

▷ Sew one vertically cut sashing piece to each long side of the pieced blocks.

▷ Use the diagram below as a guide to stitch your blocks together into rows. Press all seams toward the sashing pieces.

▷ Sew a 2" x 11 ½" inner border piece to the left side of Basket Blocks C and H. Sew a 2" x 11 ½" inner border piece to the right side of Basket Blocks E and J.

▷ You should have 6 horizontally cut sashing pieces remaining at this point. You will use these for the top and bottom sashings.

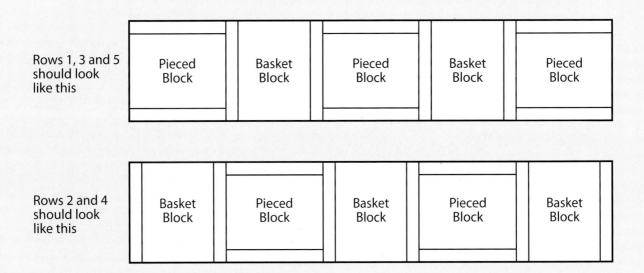

Rows 1, 3 and 5 should look like this — Pieced Block, Basket Block, Pieced Block, Basket Block, Pieced Block

Rows 2 and 4 should look like this — Basket Block, Pieced Block, Basket Block, Pieced Block, Basket Block

Top and Bottom Sashing

To make the final part of the sashing, stitch the following pieces together to make the top and bottom rows. The inner border pieces and sashing pieces are all the same size but cut from different fabrics. Make two of these, one for the top row of sashing and one for the bottom row of sashing.

Stitch the rows of your quilt together in the order shown in the Basket Quilt Layout Diagram on page 29.

Attach the top and bottom sashings.

2"	Inner Border	Sashing	Inner Border	Sashing	Inner Border	2"

Top and Bottom Sashing Guide

Pieced Block 1	Basket A	Pieced Block 2	Basket B	Pieced Block 3
Basket C	Pieced Block 4	Basket D	Pieced Block 5	Basket E
Pieced Block 6	Basket F	Pieced Block 7	Basket G	Pieced Block 8
Basket H	Pieced Block 9	Basket I	Pieced Block 10	Basket J
Pieced Block 11	Basket K	Pieced Block 12	Basket L	Pieced Block 13

Inner Border - Corner Squares

It is time to gather together some of the pieces that you cut and set aside. You will need the 12 – 2" squares of sashing fabric, 8 – 2" square of inner border fabric, and 8 – 2" x 3 ½" rectangles inner border fabric.

Following the diagram below, stitch the squares and rectangles into rows, pressing the seams (where possible) toward the dark squares to construct the inner border. Please note that the diagrams are not to scale. Set these aside.

Before you trim your borders, please check that your quilt measures 58 ½" square. If it measures larger or smaller than this, adjust the measurements shown to the size of your quilt.

Side Borders

Sew two strips together along the 5" side; press the seam to one side and trim to measure 58 ½" long. Pin and stitch the side border to one side of your quilt. Repeat for the second side. Press seams toward the border.

Top and Bottom Borders

Sew two strips together along the 5" side. Press the seam to one side and trim to measure 58 ½" long. You now need to stitch the corner squares to the ends of each border strip. Stitch the Top Left corner square to the top border, and then stitch the Top Right corner square to the right hand end. Aligning the seams and raw edges, stitch this top inner border to your quilt.

Repeat this step for the bottom border, making sure you have the corner square blocks in the correct orientation so the dark squares all point out towards the corner of the quilt. Press seams towards the border.

Outer Border

Measure the height of your quilt top across the middle. It should now measure 67 ½".

Side Borders

Sew 2 outer border strips together along the 2" side. Press the seam to one side and trim to measure 67" ½" long (or the height of your quilt). Pin the first strip to one side of your quilt, aligning the raw edges, and stitch in place using a ¼" seam allowance. Repeat for the second side. Press seams toward the border.

Top and Bottom Borders:

Now measure your quilt across the center. It should measure 70 ½".

Sew 2 outer border strips together along the 2" side. Press the seam to one side and trim to measure 70 ½" (or the width of your quilt). Pin to the top of your quilt, aligning the raw edges, and stitch in place using a ¼" seam allowance. Repeat this step on the bottom of the quilt. Press seams toward the border.

Quilting

Quilt using your preferred method. Mine was machine quilted using an all over water pattern and ditch stitching around the baskets, adding some definition stitching where necessary to emphasize the basket and flower designs. The border was quilted with a floral pattern in a scroll-type design. You could achieve the same look by hand or machine.

Binding

The Japanese Woven (textured) fabrics are much thicker than normal printed cottons, so a single binding gives a beautiful finish with a woven fabric. However, if you prefer to use print fabric, I suggest using a double binding. I recommend using a walking foot for either type of binding.

Lay your first strip right side up. Place your second strip right side down at right angles and stitch across the diagonal as shown below (Diagram A). Repeat this until you have all nine pieces sewn into a long strip. Trim away the excess fabric in the seam allowance, so the seam allowance is now ¼", Press the seam allowance open.

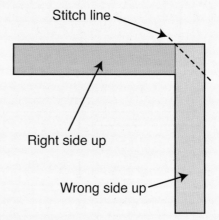

Stitch line

Right side up

Wrong side up

Pressing

Lay your binding strip on your ironing board wrong side up. Fold and press in half, down the long length, so that the cut edges meet and your strip now measures ⅞" wide (first crease line). Now open the binding strip and fold and press the raw edge toward the middle crease that you made in the previous step. Repeat for the other raw edge. You will now have a single binding with both raw edges in the middle (outer crease lines) and your binding will measure approximately ⁷⁄₁₆" (just under ½" inch) when folded closed.

Attaching the binding to your Quilt:

Align the raw edge as indicated on the right of the diagram below with the outer edge of your quilt with the binding open and the right side against your quilt. Using your walking foot, stitch along the outer crease line (the one closest to the edge of your quilt).

Stitch the binding on in the same manner you would a double binding. Once stitched in place, fold the binding over to the back of your quilt folding under the seam allowance at the second outer crease and slip stitch the binding along the outer crease line to the back of your quilt.

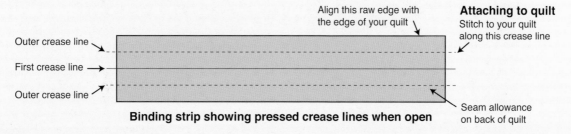

Align this raw edge with the edge of your quilt

Attaching to quilt
Stitch to your quilt along this crease line

Outer crease line

First crease line

Outer crease line

Seam allowance on back of quilt

Binding strip showing pressed crease lines when open

Basket Pillow Cover

FINISHED SIZE: 12" X 14"

Pillow covers are a great way to finish a quilt destined for a bed, or to coordinate it with your furniture if it is to be draped over a sofa or chair or displayed in a living area. They are relatively simple to make and look great as a project on their own, or as a group of pillows displayed beautifully on a sofa.

Fabric and Supplies

▷ Selection of fat eighths or scraps for appliqué

▷ Fat quarter for appliqué background

▷ ¼ yard for border

▷ ½ yard for backing

▷ ½ yard of Fusible Batting

▷ Polyfil Stuffing or pillow form

Cutting Instructions

▷ Appliqué background: cut 1 – 10" x 12" rectangle; this will be trimmed to 8 ½" x 10 ½" once you have completed the appliqué.

▷ Borders: cut 2 – 2 ½" x 10 ½" rectangles for side borders and 2 – 2 ½" x 12 ½" rectangles for the top and bottom borders.

▷ Back: 2 – 12 ½" x 10" rectangles.

Sewing Instructions

Front

It's a good idea to mark (with pins or a disappearing pen) the 8 ½" x 10 ½" area that the background fabric will be trimmed down to so that you can ensure your appliquéd basket is at least ½" inside the edge.

Choose a basket appliqué from the quilt basket templates on pages 74-86. Appliqué in place using your preferred method.

Trim away the background from behind the appliqué leaving a ¼" seam allowance around all the pieces. Press and trim the background fabric to 8 ½" wide x 10 ½" tall.

Add the side borders first, pressing the seams toward the outer edge of the cushion. Add the top and bottom borders, and again, press the seams toward the outside.

Quilting

If you want to quilt the top of your pillow cover, you should do so now before the back is attached. I like to use fusible batting as it is usually very stable and won't move, keeping the pillow front in shape while you quilt. I quilted in the ditch around the basket and the border seams, and you could do as little or as much quilting as you desire.

Pillow Back

This type of backing makes a pocket back and overlaps at the back of the cushion.

Fold one of the 10" sides on both backing pieces over ¼" twice so that the raw edge is hidden. Top stitch a scant ¼" in from the edge of the fold to finish the edge. If you want to add a closure, such as buttons or Velcro, then you will need to do so at this point. I find the overlap gives a nice finish, but if you like your cushions very full, then I recommend using a button closure.

If I am adding buttons, I sew two buttons holes about 2" to 2 ½" either side of the center on one 10" edge of the backing. I wait until the cushion is completed to add the buttons so I can line them up perfectly.

Lay your cushion front right side up. Lay one backing piece right side down on top of the cushion front, aligning the raw edges with the cushion front at the top of the cushion (this would be the piece of backing with button holes in it). The seamed edge should be near the middle of the cushion as shown. Pin and stitch around the pillow on the three sides using ¼" seams.

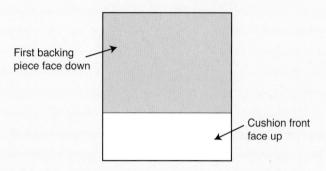

First backing piece face down

Cushion front face up

Repeat for the second backing piece but align the edges at the bottom of the cushion. The backing pieces should overlap where you have hemmed the edges.

Turn the pillow right side out through the opening in the back. Poke out the corners if necessary and then press so it is nice and rectangular. Top stitch ½" from the finished edge to make the Oxford edge of the cushion. I like this method, as I find piping a cushion can be fiddly, and this looks really nice on most cushions and gives the cushion a nice finish.

Tip: Oxford Edge

If you want to make the Oxford edge wider on your cushion (up to 2" can look really good) just adjust the size of your outer border and backing pieces accordingly, and make your top stitching wider so the inner part of the cushion remains the same but the Oxford edge is wider. A wider Oxford edge is especially nice on a large cushion or pillow sham for a bed.

Insert your cushion into the cover to finish. Pin and stitch a ¼" seam around all four sides.

If you would like to make a hanging rather than a pillow, you can add a single backing rather than the overlap-style backing. Simply cut the backing the same size as the front. Lay the appliquéd top and the back right sides together. Stitch around the edge using a ¼" seam and leaving a gap at the bottom for turning right side out. Trim the corners and turn right side out; press and slipstitch the opening closed.

I also like to top stitch the edge of a hanging to make it look like piping. To do this, stitch about ¼" in from the edge around all four sides.

In the hanging shown here, the center has been trimmed to 7 ½" x 9 ½" to suit the basket and it has a ½" finished (1" cut) inner border and a 1 ½" finished (2" cut) outer border.

Taupe About Town Bag

FINISHED SIZE: 10" X 12" X 2" (EXCLUDING HANDLE)

This is a really fun bag to make that is great as a handbag about town, or for carrying your projects to class. I used a roll of 2 ½" strips to make this bag, or you could use a mix of fabrics and one piece for the back and lining.

Fabric and Supplies

▷ Selection of fabrics cut into 2 ½" strips (at least 16 different fabrics will give a nice variety of colors and patterns for the bag fabric)

▷ ½ yard for the lining

▷ ½ yard of Fusible Batting

▷ Cosmo Embroidery thread: (I used 467 and 923)

▷ Wooden or plastic handles

Cutting Instructions

From your 2 ½" strips select or cut the following:

▷ 1 – 2 ½" x 40" strip for the handle loops

▷ 2 – 2½" x 10 ½" rectangles and 1 – 2 ½" x 12 ½" strip for the bag base and sides

▷ 6 – 2 ½" x 10 ½" strips for the back

▷ 10 – 2 ½" squares and 20 – 1 ½" x 4 ½" strips for the front

▷ 1 – 2 ½" x 40" strip for the binding

For the lining cut:

▷ 2 – 10 ½" x 12 ½" rectangles for the back and front

▷ 2 – 2 ½" x 10 ½" strips for the sides

▷ 1 – 2 ½" x 12 ½" strips for the base

Sewing Instructions

Front

Following the layout diagram on page 88, lay out your smaller rectangles and squares in a pleasing color arrangement. Stitch these together into columns and then join the columns to make the bag front. Press seams to one side as you go to make the bag as flat as possible.

Trace the flower outline (from page 90) onto the bag front and using two strands of embroidery thread, embroider the flowers using the backstitch (see page 6).

Tip: You can add as many or few flowers in varying colors to personalize the bag.

Back

Following the diagram on page 87, stitch the six back pieces together to make a rectangle. Trim if necessary so that both the front and the back pieces are the same size.

Stitch the sides to the front, stopping ¼" before the bottom of the bag, Make a back stich or lock stitch at this point so that the seam does not come undone. Stitch the base to the bottom of the front starting and stopping ¼" from each end. Stitch the back of the bag to the bag base starting and stopping ¼" from each end. Your bag will now be one flat piece.

Fuse the batting to the wrong side of the outside fabric and quilt as desired, including the bottom. Quilting the bottom of the bag makes it sturdier.

Putting the bag together

With right sides together, sew the sides to the back using a ¼" seam allowance and stopping ¼" from the bottom. Bring the bottom of the side piece and the bottom of the bag together, right sides facing. This will be an odd shape as you started and stopped sewing ¼" in from the edge on the bottom seams, but it will allow the base seam to come together with the side. Stitch across the base to close each bottom edge of the bag. Repeat this for the lining, using a ½" seam. Because the outer bag is quilted and thickened by the batting, a ½" seam allowance is needed on the lining; otherwise the lining will be too big.

Insert the bag lining into the main bag, wrong sides together. Pin in place so the top edges are aligned.

Binding

Fold the binding in half, wrong sides together, so that it now measures 1 ¼" wide; press. Just as you would bind a quilt, lay the binding right side against the outside of the bag so that the raw edges are aligned with the top edge of the bag. Turn under the raw edge on one end of the binding. Stitch the binding around the top edge starting about 1" from the folded end and using a ¼" seam. Stop before you get to the beginning. Trim the binding, allowing about ½" to tuck into the beginning of the binding. Tuck the raw edge into the folded edge and continue sewing. Roll the binding over to the lining side and slipstitch in place.

Attaching the handles

To make the handle loops, take your 2 ½" x 40" strip and, with right sides together, sew down the length of the strip to make a tube. Turn right side out and press so the seam is in the middle of the tube. Cut into 4 – 8" strips. Thread each strip through the openings on the handles. Pin the loops in place folding under approximately 1" on each end and attaching them 1" down from the top edge of the bag inline with your bag handles. Slip stitch in place on three sides to firmly attach the handles and hide the turned under edges of the loops.

Tip: Add a sew-in magnetic snap to close your bag and/or add a decorative button for a personal touch.

Petal Basket Bag

FINISHED SIZE: 6" WIDE X 6 ¾" TALL INCLUDING THE HANDLE

This is such a simple bag that is perfect for keeping bits and pieces in, giving as a gift or just as a nice sewing room tidy. As a variation you could make it with one beautiful fabric rather than using strip pieces. I can never choose just one fabric so I usually end up with twenty different fabrics, which means you can make each side different.

Fabric and Supplies

▷ 1 fat quarter or a selection of 20 fabrics that are at least 1 ½" x 7"

▷ 1 fat quarter for bag lining and bag lining base (you can use 2 fat eighths for this if you use a different fabric for the inside base lining.) When selecting your lining keep in mind that the lining forms the top edge of the bag.

▷ 1 fat eighth for the bag handle

▷ ½ yard of Fusible Batting

Cutting Instructions

From the batting cut:

▷ 1 round base (templates on page 89)

▷ 1 – 4" x 16" strip for the handle

▷ 1 – 6 ¾" x 20 ½" piece for the main bag

From the lining/contrast fabric cut:

▷ 2 round bases (page 89)

▷ 1 – 7 ¾" x 19 ½" rectangle for the lining

▷ 1 – 4" x 16" rectangle for the handle

For the exterior of the bag cut 20 – 1 ½" x 7" strips

Sewing Instructions

To make the pieced exterior of the bag, arrange the 20 strips in a pleasing color and tone arrangement. Strips 5 and 6, counting in from each end, will form the center front and center back of the bag, so I like to put my favorite fabrics in these positions. Stitch each piece to the next using a ¼" seam allowance and pressing the seams in one direction after each strip is attached.

▷ Trim to 20 ½" x 6 ¾".

Appliqué

If you are going to appliqué on top of the strips you should do this now using your preferred method using the octagon and Petal Pincushion patterns on page 89. It is a good idea to mark where your center front will be so that you know where to place the appliqué.

Fuse the batting to the wrong side of the bag base, exterior fabric piece, and to the bag handle fabric. A silicon appliqué pressing sheet is helpful for this step. Quilt the bag and the base as desired at this point. I recommend quilting in the ditch of each strip and around the appliqué design. Several lines of quilting across the base will make it nice and firm when it is stitched to the bag.

Fold the handle in half along the length, right sides together. Stitch all the way around leaving a 3" to 4" opening along one long side for turning. Turn right side out, press, and then slip stitch the opening closed. Top stitch all the way around, ¼" in from the edge.

Stitch the short sides of the pieced outer rectangle

together, right sides facing. Pin to the round base with right sides together and stitch using a ¼" seam allowance, easing as necessary. Repeat for the lining. Put the lining inside the bag, wrong sides together. Fold the excess lining over ½" twice towards the outside of the bag to form a binding around the top. Slip stitch in place.

Pin your handle in place on opposite sides. I like to hide the side seam at the top. Stitch to secure the handle in place.

Tip: To personalize your bag, you could add buttons at the base of the handle, or add some decorative embroidery on the appliqué.

40

Tumbling Blocks Pincushion

FINISHED SIZE: 4" SQUARE X 1 ½" HIGH

J love pincushions. They are fun to make and they make great gifts, as you can spend time embellishing them or picking the perfect color and fabrics for the recipient. And you can never have too many pincushions. They make fabulous decorations that are also practical for everyday use.

This is a fun little pincushion that you can make from scraps or just a few fabrics. The tumbling blocks always remind me of little baskets (without handles of course) and they always look so nice whether made from shades of one color or with higher contrasting fabrics.

Fabric and Supplies

▷ Scraps of fabric for the tumbling blocks, the equivalent of 24 – 2" squares

▷ 1 – fat eighth for the sides and bottom

▷ 5" square of thin batting

▷ Polyfil Stuffing

Cutting Instructions

▷ Cut 24 tumbling blocks from your selected fabrics using templates A and B on page 93, which are identical with B being the upside down version of A

▷ Cut 1 – 4 ½" square for the bottom

▷ Cut 4 – 4 ½" x 2" strips for the sides

Sewing Instructions

Lay the tumbling block pieces out in a pleasing color arrangement so that you have 4 rows of 6 tumbling blocks each. Every other block will be upside down, so, using the direction of the templates, the first row will be A, B, A, B, A, B, and the second row will be B, A, B, A, B, A and so on. You will know if you have them the

wrong way up because when sewn together they will make a curve rather than a straight row.

Stitch each block in the row to the next using a ¼" seam allowance. Press the first row seams to one side. Repeat for the next rows, pressing the seam allowances in alternate directions.

Stitch the rows together, aligning the seams and pressing the seam allowances as you go. Your completed tumbling blocks top won't be exactly square, because of the shape of the tumblers. The top and bottom edges will be a straight line, but the sides will go in and out because of the angles of the tumbler block sides (see diagram). The top may measure slightly less than 4 ½" in width at the narrowest parts of the sides. Don't worry about this, as narrow pieces will be in the seam allowance.

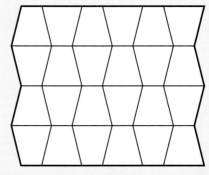

Fuse or pin your tumbling block top to a 5" square piece of batting. Quilt as desired (I stitched in the ditch). Trim the batting and top to 4 ½" square. On the two sides where the tumbling blocks are angled, make sure that the batting is showing equally on each side. Provided you have ⅛" of fabric in the seam allowance, your pincushion will be secure once made. If you are concerned that the edges may move during construction or in use, you can stay stitch along the two angled sides a scant ⅛" in from the raw fabric edges to keep them in place.

Using a ¼" seam allowance, stitch the 4 sides to the pincushion top starting and stopping ¼" in from each edge. (See the instructions for the Triangle Pincushion on page 55 for more details.)

After all four sides are attached, stitch the side seams starting at the point where you stopped sewing, ¼" in from the edge.

Pin and stitch the base to the sides, leaving a small opening along one side (not at a corner) to enable you to turn the pincushion right side out. Stuff firmly and slip stitch the opening closed.

Tip: If you have a locking stitch on your sewing machine, it is helpful to use this at the ¼" stopping and starting points when you are sewing the sides of the pincushion.

Petal Pin Cushion

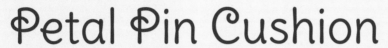

FINISHED SIZE APPROXIMATELY 5" SQUARE

Fabric and Supplies

▷ A selection of fabric scraps for petals

▷ Two squares at least 5 ½" in size for the back and front

▷ Decorative ribbon (optional)

▷ Polyfil Stuffing

Cutting Instructions

▷ Cut 2 – 5 ½" squares, one for the pincushion top and one for the back.

Sewing Instructions

Fold your pincushion front fabric in half and press; fold in half again so you make two perpendicular press lines (and the pincushion front now shows four segments). Use these press lines to assist you with centering the flower petal appliqué design on your pincushion top, using the flower appliqué on page 89.

Appliqué the petals and center in place using your preferred method. Trim away any excess fabric under the appliqué so that you have a ¼" seam underneath. This helps the petals to puff up when the pincushion is stuffed.

If you want to quilt the pincushion top you can do so now, but I prefer not to as I think they look best just appliquéd.

Stitch along the center of one edge of the front a scant ¼" from the edge. Repeat this on the back of the pincushion. This will help you to know where the pincushion should be left open once it is sewn and stuffed. Lay your pincushion top right side up. Lay the pincushion back right side down, with the two stitch lines on the same side. Pin and stitch a ¼" seam around all the sides leaving an opening on the side you have already put the stitched line.

Trim the corners and turn the pincushion right side out. Stuff to the firmness you like. Pin the opening closed. Using the scant ¼" stitch lines as a guide, slipstitch the opening closed.

If you would like to add the ribbon trim, fold it in half and pin it to the back of the pincushion on one corner. Tuck under approximately ¼" to ½" at the raw ends so that they are hidden once you slipstitch the ribbon in place.

Tip: If you would like to personalize the pincushion you can add a braid around the seam edge or a button over the petal center. When attaching the button, stitch right though the pincushion so that the center is indented. This also makes the sides firmer.

Basket Needle Case

FINISHED SIZE: 6 ½" X 4 ½"

Needle cases are fun to make and they don't take much fabric, so you can often make them using fabric leftover from other projects. Or, if you are like me, you can start a whole new collection of fabric to make the perfect needle case for a gift. I like to use wool for the needle keep, as this preserves your needles in nice condition and they won't slip out.

Fabric and Supplies

- ▷ 1 – fat eighth or scraps for the border and back
- ▷ 1 – fat eighth or scraps for the pocket and appliqué
- ▷ 1 – fat eighth for appliqué
- ▷ 1 – fat eighth for lining
- ▷ Fusible Batting: ¼ yard or scrap
- ▷ Wool: 6" square
- ▷ Cosmo Embroidery thread (I used numbers 235, 368, 652 and 369)

Cutting Instructions

- ▷ Appliqué Background: 6" x 7" (this will be trimmed down later)
- ▷ Front Borders: 2 – 1" x 6" strips and 2 – 1" x 5" strips
- ▷ Bias for basket handle: 1" x 7" (folded into thirds lengthwise)
- ▷ Back: 7" x 9 ¼"
- ▷ Lining and batting: 7" x 13 ¾"
- ▷ Pocket: 7" x 9 ½"
- ▷ Wool: 5 ½" x 3 ¼"

Sewing Instructions

Front

Using your preferred method, appliqué the basket and handle on page 90 onto the background fabric. Trace the embroidered flowers and words onto the appliqué and the background fabric. Use two strands of Cosmo embroidery thread to complete the embroidery (refer to the stitch guide on page 6 for details of the stitches). The flowers are made up of backstitch and French knots.

Trim the appliqué background to measure 4" wide by 6" tall. Stitch the 1" x 6" border strips to each side of the background; press seams toward the outside. Stitch the back rectangle to the left side of the front appliqué border to complete the front/outside of the needlecase. Stitch the top 1" x 5" borders in place; press seams toward the outside. Fuse the batting to the wrong side of the needle case front. Quilt the front if desired at this point. I top stitched ¼" around the outer edge of the basket and quilted in the ditch around the basket and in the ditch around the border.

Pocket

Press the pocket rectangle in half, right sides together, to make a 3 ½" x 9 ½" rectangle. With the fold at the top, stitch a ¼" seam down the right-hand edge. Clip the top corner of the side you just stitched and turn right side out; press again. Topstitch ¼" down from the folded edge along the length.

Lining

Place the pocket on the bottom left-hand corner of the lining with right sides together so that the raw edges are even. Tack in place using a scant ¼" seam along the left side and lower edges. The fold will be halfway up the lining and the seamed edge will be two-thirds of the way across the length of the lining. Top stitch the right hand edge of the pocket to the lining a scant ⅛" away from the edge of the pocket.

Fold the wool rectangle in half and position it in place on the last third of the needle case lining, so that it is centered in the area, allowing for the ¼" seam allowance. Open out and pin in place. Stitch down the fold line of the wool to secure it to the lining fabric.

Putting it all together

With rights sides together, stitch the lining to the appliquéd front, including the batting. Stitch around all the edges leaving a 3" to 4" opening along the top edge for turning through. Clip the corners and turn right side out. Slipstitch the opening closed. Topstitch ¼" all the way around the edge of the needle case.

Fold the needle case into thirds. The front and middle sections should measure 4 ½" wide and the final section should measure 4 ¼" wide. Mark these folds and top stitch along these fold lines, starting and stopping ¼" from the top and bottom edge so that you do not stitch past the topstitching.

To secure the needle case, I used sew-in magnetic snap. You could also use regular snaps or Velcro, but I like the way the sew-in magnetic snaps literally "snap" together when you close the needle case.

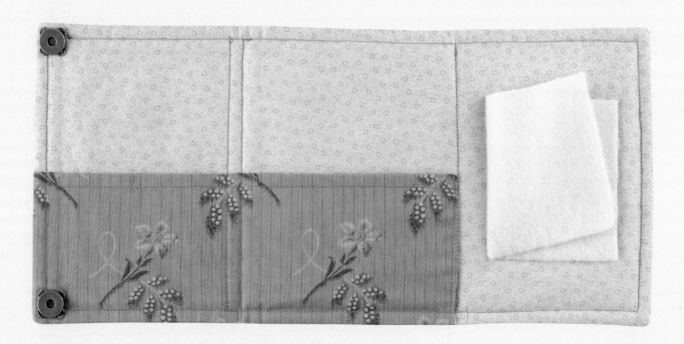

Basket Notebook Cover

FINISHED SIZE: 8 ½" X 6"

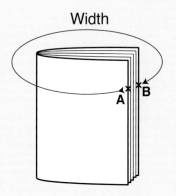
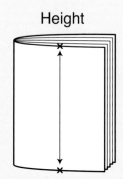

Width

Height

Jf you have my first book, "Taupe Inspirations," you know I love notebook covers and this pretty cover takes things a step further. The cute little basket on the front is actually a pocket to put your needles or little sewing scissors in. So not only is it pretty, it's also functional. I have worked out a formula so that you can use any size notebook or binder, as they can vary considerably in depth even if the front size is the same.

Fabric and Supplies

Note: Yardage given here is for an 8 ½" x 6" notebook. See the instructions for determining yardage needed for a different sized notebook.

▷ Cover: 1 – fat quarter to ½ yard

▷ Lining: 1 – fat quarter to ½ yard

▷ Appliqué: Scraps or 1 – fat eighth for basket and handle

▷ Basket Background: 1 – fat eighth

▷ Cosmo Embroidery thread (I used #233, 235 and 368)

▷ Fusible batting: ½ yard

▷ Notebook/binder: 8 ½" x 6"

How to determine yardage for other binder sizes

To determine the size fabric you will need, first measure the size of your binder. Measure from the top to bottom of your binder to obtain the height. To obtain the width, measure around your binder using a flexible tape measure starting at the right hand edge of the front cover and finishing at the same point on the back cover. It is best to measure the width when your binder is closed to allow enough fabric to have a good tuck-in at each end.

Compute the size fabric pieces you need using the following formula:

> Your height measurement + 1" =
> Height of fabric
>
> Your width measurement + 6 ½" =
> Width of fabric

For example, a nice size binder that will fit easily in your quilt bag or handbag is 10 ½" high with a total width of 16 ¾" (7 ¾" across the front + 1 ¼" across the spine + 7 ¾" across the back). To make a cover for this size binder you would calculate the following:

▷ 10 ½" + 1" = 11 ½"

▷ 16 ¾" + 6 ½" = 23 ¼"

Thus you will cut 1 rectangle that is 11 ½" x 23 ¼" from the batting, the lining fabric and the cover fabric.

Tip: The width measurement is less critical, so I would round this measurement up to the next ½" or 1" to make cutting a little easier.

Sewing Instructions

Basket

Trace the basket template on page 91 onto freezer paper. Cut two of these from your basket fabric and one from fusible batting.

Iron the fusible batting onto the wrong side of one of the basket pieces; remember to iron on the fabric, not the batting, as it can melt onto your iron. Use an appliqué pressing sheet if you have one. Lay the second basket piece on top with right sides facing each other.

Stitch around all sides, leaving an opening of approximately 2" on one side so that you can turn the basket through. Clip the corners and turn right side out. Slipstitch the opening closed. Top stitch a scant ⅛" on the top edge only.

From the same basket fabric, cut a bias strip 1" wide by approximately 8" long. Fold the strip in approximately ¼" on one long side. Repeat for the other long side so that you have folded the bias strip approximately in thirds. Press the bias handle into a rough curve. This will help later when you are pinning it into place.

Oval Background

Trace the oval background template (page 92) onto freezer paper. Position this oval on the right side of your background fabric and press in place. Cut around the template ¼" to ½" outside the drawn line for your seam allowance. Remove the freezer paper and place it on the wrong side of the fabric, paper side against the fabric and shiny side up. Press the seam allowance over onto the freezer paper so that you have a nice smooth edge for your oval background.

Putting the front together

To determine exactly where your background oval should be appliquéd, wrap the outer fabric around the notebook as if you have already made the outside cover, making sure that the excess fabric is tucked evenly inside the front and back. Mark with pins or chalk the front edge of the spine and front tuck points. You will position your oval evenly spaced between these marks.

Pin the oval in place and appliqué onto the cover fabric. Using the layout guide on page 91, position your basket and handle on the oval, pin in place. Appliqué the basket handle all the way around. Starting at the point on the basket where the inside of the handle meets the basket, top stitch a scant ⅛" from the basket edge all the way around the basket, but leaving the basket open between the handles. This forms the pocket.

Trace the embroidery design onto the oval and complete the embroidery using 2 strands of Cosmo embroidery floss. The stems and leaves are stitched in backstitch and the flower centers are made of French knots (refer to stitch guide on page 6 for details of these stitches).

Tip: If you wish to add more flowers you can. I recommend you add them in pairs, as flowers always look better in odd numbers.

Assembling the Cover

Fuse the batting to the wrong side of the outer fabric rectangle. Use an appliqué pressing sheet if you have one so that the batting does not stick to your iron. Lay the lining fabric on top of the outer fabric, right sides together.

Tip: Use the grid marks on your cutting mat to align one side edge and the top edge. Trim off any excess before sewing

Stitch around all sides using a ¼" seam and leaving an opening of about 3" on one of the short sides, preferably the back cover side. Turn right side out and slip stitch the opening closed. Press the notebook cover so it is nice and flat.

If you want to top stitch or quilt the notebook cover, you should do so at this point. Wrap the padded rectangle around your notebook and fold the excess inside the front and back covers at the points you marked earlier. If you need to move these marks, do so now, making sure that the cover design is centered and the folded flaps are even at the front and back of the book.

Slipstitch the folded flaps together, along both the top and bottom edge (this is the part that you tucked inside the front and back covers). You can remove the notebook for this step or clothes pegs are great for holding the flaps in place if you keep the notebook in place while you are stitching.

Sewing Case

FINISHED SIZE APPROXIMATELY 9 ½" X 6" X 2" DEEP

This type of sewing case is very popular in Japan and not only looks pretty once covered, but is also very useful. Once I started using mine, I didn't want to part with it, so I hope you enjoy using yours as much as I do. The pockets inside are a really good size and the triangle pincushion can be removed while you are sewing. This bag is relatively new outside of Japan, so if you cannot find one in your local store, please e-mail me as I try to keep them in stock all the time.

Fabric and Supplies

▷ Selection of fat eighths or scraps for appliqué and triangles

▷ 1 – fat quarter for appliqué background, pincushion base, sides and borders around the triangle pocket (on back of bag)

▷ ¼ yard of Fusible Batting

▷ Polyfil Stuffing

▷ Curved Upholstery Needle

▷ Cosmo Embroidery thread (I used #236)

▷ Purchased sewing case

Cutting Instructions

From the fusible batting: 2 – 6 ½" x 10" and 4 ½" x 10"

For the back pocket cut 30 triangles from assorted fabrics - I used a Creative Grids 60 degree triangle ruler and 2" strips, or you can use the template on page 53.

From the background fabric cut:

▷ 1 – 8" x 11" piece for appliqué background

▷ 2 – 2" x 21" strips for the pocket side borders

▷ 2 – 1 ½" x 21" strips for the top and bottom pocket borders

Sewing Instructions

Pocket

Stitch the triangles into 2 rows of 15 triangles each using the picture as a guide and using a 1/4" seam allowance. Stitch the rows together, press and trim to measure approximately 8 1/2" x 3 1/4"; your measurement may vary depending on how it fits your pocket. Add the 2" borders to each side of the pocket triangles.

Trace around the pocket side of your case and make a paper template as each case may vary slightly. Square off one long side of the template for the pocket top. Cut batting the same size as this pocket template and fuse to the wrong side of your triangle pocket piece. Cut your pocket 1/2" to 3/4" larger all the way around than your batting. Quilt as desired. Fold under the seam allowance but don't press it.

Pin in place on your sewing case pocket with the top edge along the taped edge of the pocket. Tuck under the seam allowance and stitch in place using slipstitch or running stitch with a curved needle.

You will find this easier if you put your fingers into the pocket to help stretch the pocket away from the main case. You will make the running stitch in two steps: First make the stitch into the case, pull the needle and thread through, and then make the stitch into the pocket cover and pull the thread through, then make the next stitch into the case. Take your time and try to stretch open the piped edge so that you get the pocket cover as far down into the seam crease of the pocket as you can. When you then let the case relax, your seam edge will be hidden by the piping.

Front

Appliqué the flower on page 92 onto the background fabric using your preferred method. Trace and embroider the words using a backstitch and two strands of Cosmo embroidery thread.

Trace the oval template for the front of the sewing case on page 92. Before you cut this out, check it against your sewing case to make sure it fits, and adjust the size if needed by drawing larger or smaller lines around the oval to fit the top of your sewing case. This will be the size without a seam allowance.

Once you are happy with your template, cut it out. Pin the template onto your front fabric and cut around your template leaving a ½" to ¾" seam all the way around. Cut an oval from the batting using the same template but without adding a seam allowance. Press and fuse the wadding to the wrong side of the front cover fabric, centering it so that you have an even seam allowance on all the sides.

Stitch in place using a curved needle as per the pocket.

To complete your case, make the Triangle Pincushion on page 55 for the inside of the case.

Tip: you can personalize the bag by adding your name or own words to the sewing case. The case comes with a beige side (as shown) or black outer edge (the cover colors vary but as you cover these it doesn't matter which color you get). The black is nice and gives a different look to the Taupe colored case I have used.

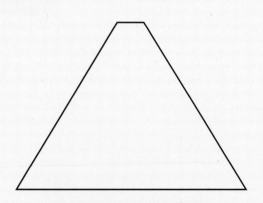

**Triangle template for
Triangle Pin Cushion**

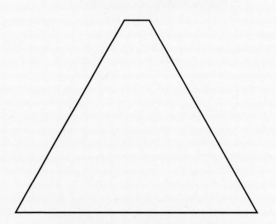

**Triangle template for
back of Sewing Case**

Triangle Pincushion

FINISHED SIZE: 9 ½" AT BACK, 8" AT FRONT AND 1" DEEP

This pincushion fits neatly into the compartment next to the hinged side of the sewing case. The divider inside the bag can be adjusted so you want to move the long divider to make a narrow space to fit the pincushion. It looks cute on its own, but it really finishes off the sewing case.

Fabric and Supplies

▷ Scraps of fabric for the triangles

▷ 1 –fat eighth for sides and base

▷ Polyfil Stuffing

Cutting Instructions

Triangles: cut 11 using the template on page 53

▷ 1 – 1 ½" x 8 ½" strip for narrower front

▷ 1 – 1 ½" x 10" strip for longer back

▷ 2 – 1 ½" x 2" strips for each end

▷ 1 – 1 ½" x 10" strip for the base (trim to same size as top before sewing the sides on)

Sewing Instructions

Lay out your triangles into a pleasing color arrangement. Stitch each one to the next with side seams aligned. Press seams to one side as you go.

To make sure your base piece matches your top perfectly, lay your pieced triangle top on top of the base piece (wrong sides together). Trim your base piece to match your top.

Using a ¼" seam allowance, stitch the front and back sides to the triangle top starting and stopping ¼" in from each end. Attach the end pieces to the top, again starting and stopping ¼" from the ends. You may need to trim the ends so that they line up with the front and back sides. It is a good idea to do a locking stitch at the ¼" stop and start point to make sure the seam is secure.

Once all four sides are stitched on, sew the side seams together by starting to stitch at the point where you stopped sewing at the top edge, ¼" in from the end.

Pin and stitch the base to the sides, leaving a small opening along the longest side (not at a corner) to enable you to turn the pincushion right side out. Turn and stuff firmly with Polyfil Stuffing and slip stitch the opening closed.

Tip: To make it easier to stitch the opening closed in the correct position, sew a scant ¼" stitch line on the top and base pieces where you plan to leave your opening. Once you turn it through, you can line up these stitch lines so that you know where to stitch the opening closed and have a ¼" seam allowance. If you are using a woven fabric, this technique also helps to stop the edge from fraying while you are turning the pincushion through.

Pattern and Project Binder Cover

The Pattern and Project Binder Cover is such a fun and versatile idea. I can think of endless uses for this lovely covered binder. You can keep your projects all together. Patchwork patterns could be stored in clear pockets. It could be a recipe binder or homework binder. Oh, the ideas are endless and, of course, you could personalize the words on the front to your use.

The process of making this cover is identical to making the Notebook Cover, just in a larger size. You could make it with a plain back, or a tumbling block back like in the sample.

Fabric and Supplies

Note: The yardage here is for a 13 ¼" x 18" binder. See page 58 for how to compute fabric for different sized binders. For a large binder this size, I would add 6 ½" twice to the width, so 13" in total, for the flaps.

- ▷ Cover: 1 yard (includes enough fabric for a back that is not pieced)
- ▷ Lining: 1 yard
- ▷ Tumbling Blocks (optional for back cover): assorted fat eights
- ▷ Appliqué: Scraps for flower
- ▷ Appliqué Background: 1 – fat quarter
- ▷ Cosmo Embroidery thread (I used #235)
- ▷ Fusible batting: 1 yard
- ▷ Binder: 13 ¼" x 18"

Appliqué Background

Cut one rectangle 8 ½" x 10" for the appliqué background. Using your preferred method, appliqué the flower in place (see page 94 for the appliqué and embroidery templates) and trace the embroidery words onto your background fabric.

Cut one piece of fusible batting 7 ½" x 10." Fuse this to the wrong side of the background fabric, making sure it is centered from all sides. Use an appliqué pressing sheet so that the iron doesn't touch the batting or press on the front fabric side. Fold and press the seam allowances over to the wrong side to cover the edges of the batting.

Complete the embroidery using a backstitch (refer to the stitching guide on page 6 for further details) and two strands of Cosmo embroidery thread.

Tumbling Blocks Back (optional)

If you would like to make the tumbling blocks back, you will need to cut a selection of tumbling blocks. I recommend using the Creative Grids Tumbling Blocks Ruler, or use the template on page 93. You will need approximately 18 tumbling blocks, but this will vary depending on the exact size of your binder. I used three rows for my cover, but you may need an extra row if your binder is larger, or more in each row if your binder is deeper. It is easy to cut extra if you need them.

Lay the tumbling blocks out in a pleasing arrangement; stitch them into rows, and then stitch each row together. (You will know you have enough when the rectangle you have created is at least 1" taller than your binder and the width measures half the width of your binder plus 6 ½" for the flap).

How to determine yardage for other binder sizes

To determine the size fabric you will need, first measure the size of your binder. Measure from the top to bottom of your binder to obtain the height. To obtain the width, measure around your binder using a flexible tape measure starting at the right-hand edge of the front cover and finishing at the same point on the back cover. It is best to measure the width when your binder is closed to allow enough fabric to have a good tuck-in at each end.

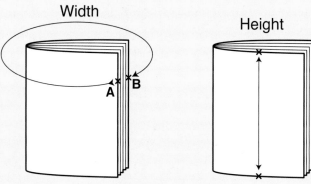

Width **Height**

Compute the size fabric pieces you need using the following formula:

> Your height measurement + 1" =
> Height of fabric
>
> Your width measurement + 13" =
> Width of fabric
>
> (If your binder is very large, you may wish to add 8"-10" to the width measurement to ensure a good tuck-in).

Tip: If you find that your cover is too big for your binder, you could make the seam allowance in the step above a little wider than ¼". You should decide this before you slipstitch the opening closed.

Putting the front together

If you have made the pieced tumbling block back, stitch it to the piece you have cut for the front (which will be one-half of the total width of the cover fabric). Use a ¼" seam to stitch the front and back together. In the sample, I used two different fabrics for the front and back lining so I stitched these together, too, using a ¼" seam allowance.

To determine exactly where appliquéd rectangle should be placed on the binder cover, wrap the outer fabric around the binder as if you have already made the outside cover, making sure that the excess fabric is tucked evenly inside the front and back. Mark with pins or chalk the front edge of the spine and front tuck points. Fuse the batting to the back of the front cover. Use an appliqué pressing sheet if you have one, pressing on the fabric side so that the batting does not stick to your iron. Now position your appliqué rectangle evenly between the pins. I like to lay mine on an angle as it looks slightly quirky, and if you don't get it perfectly centered it still looks great. Topstitch a scant ⅛" in from the edge to secure the rectangle in place. Quilt as desired. The quilting will pull in the size of the front cover and so you will now need to lay your lining, right sides together, on top of the front. Trim your lining to match and pin.

Using a ¼" seam allowance, stitch around all sides of the cover leaving a 3" to 4" opening so that you are able to turn the cover through. Clip the corners and turn right side out. Slipstitch the opening closed. Press so that your cover is nice and flat.

If you would like more topstitching or quilting, you should do so at this point.

Wrap the cover around your binder and tuck the excess inside the front and back. This should be at the points you marked earlier, but the main thing is to ensure that the appliqué is centered on the front and that the cover is tucked evenly top to bottom on both the front and back, and that the front and back tucks are the same.

Slipstitch the cover flaps together along the top and bottom edges. It may be easier to remove the binder to do this, but I like to do it with the binder in place so I can make sure the cover is nice and secure over the binder. If you have some hinged clothespins or binder clips, these are useful to hold the cover in place on the binder while you stitch the flaps together.

Patterns

8" x 1½"	
	4" x 2½"
8" x 1½"	

3" x 1½"

4" x 2½"

5½" x 1½"

3" x 1½"

5½" x 1½"

5½" x 1½"

4" x 2½"

3" x 1½"

5½" x 1½"

3" x 1½"

4" x 2½"

8" x 1½"

8" x 1½"

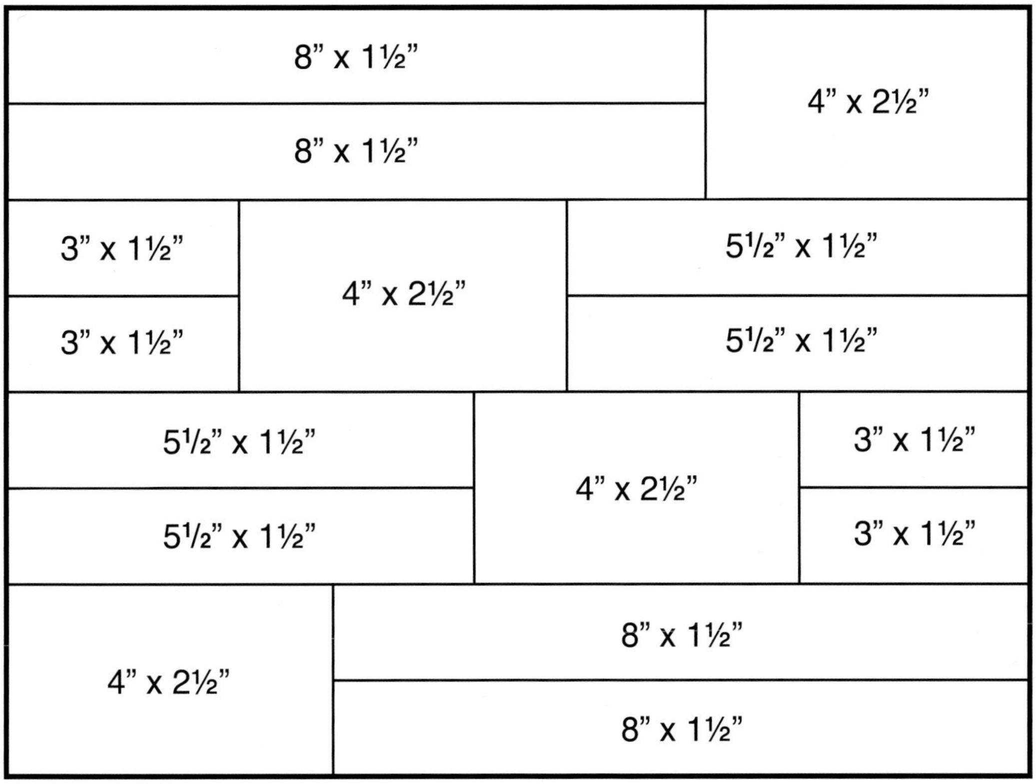

Finished block size is 11" x 8" (unfinished 11½" x 8½")

Block 2

4½" x 1½"
4½" x 1½"
4½" x 1½"
4½" x 1½"
4½" x 1½"
4½" x 1½"
4½" x 1½"
4½" x 1½"
4½" x 1½"
4½" x 1½"
4½" x 1½"
4½" x 1½"
4½" x 1½"
4½" x 1½"
4½" x 1½"
4½" x 1½"
4½" x 1½"
4½" x 1½"
4½" x 1½"
4½" x 1½"

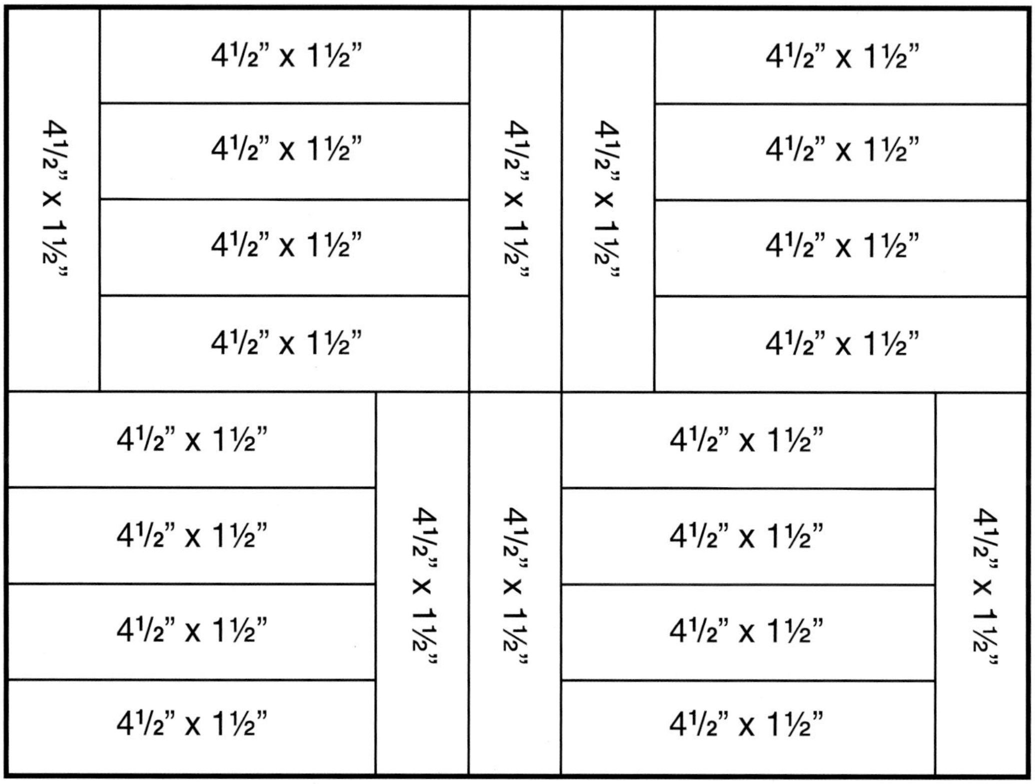

Finished block size is 11" x 8" (unfinished 11½" x 8½")

7½" x 1½"	2½" x 2½"	2½" x 2½"
7½" x 1½"		

3" x 1½"	2½" x 2½"	2½" x 2½"	5" x 1½"
3" x 1½"			5" x 1½"

5" x 1½"	2½" x 2½"	2½" x 2½"	3" x 1½"
5" x 1½"			3" x 1½"

2½" x 2½"	2½" x 2½"	7½" x 1½"
		7½" x 1½"

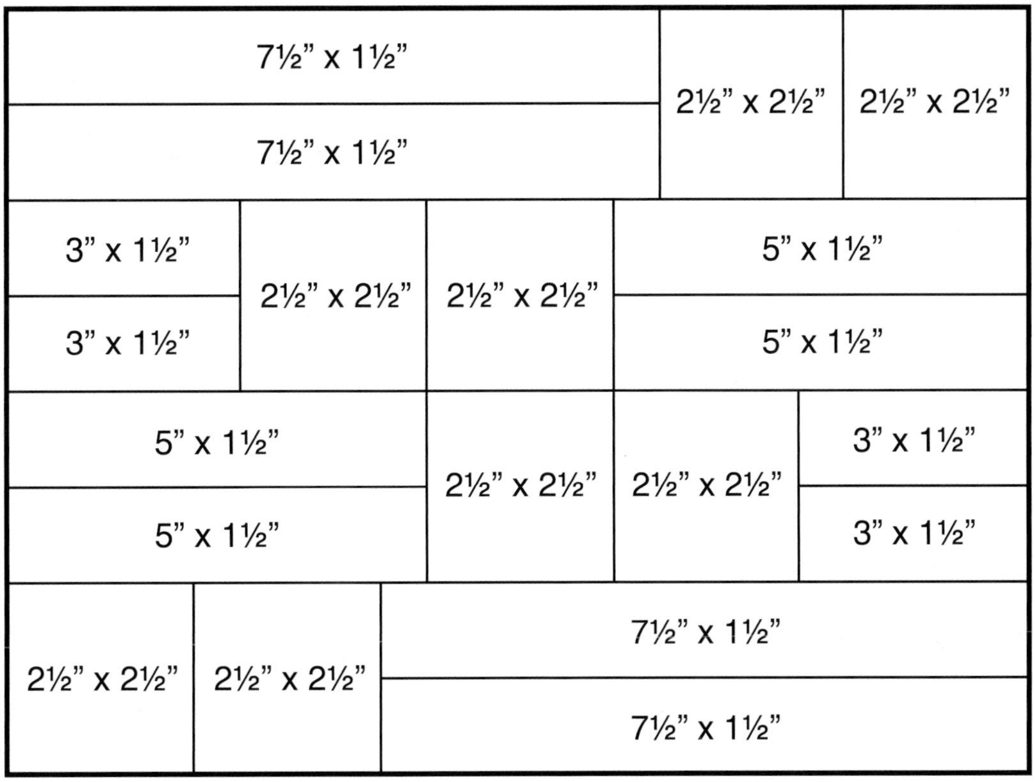

Finished block size is 11" x 8" (unfinished 11½" x 8½")

7" x 1½"		1½" x 1½"	4" x 1½"
6" x 1½"		1½" x 1½"	5" x 1½"
7" x 1½"		1½" x 1½"	4" x 1½"
5" x 1½"	1½" x 1½"	6" x 1½"	
4" x 1½"	1½" x 1½"	7" x 1½"	
6" x 1½"		1½" x 1½"	5" x 1½"
7" x 1½"		1½" x 1½"	4" x 1½"
6" x 1½"		1½" x 1½"	5" x 1½"

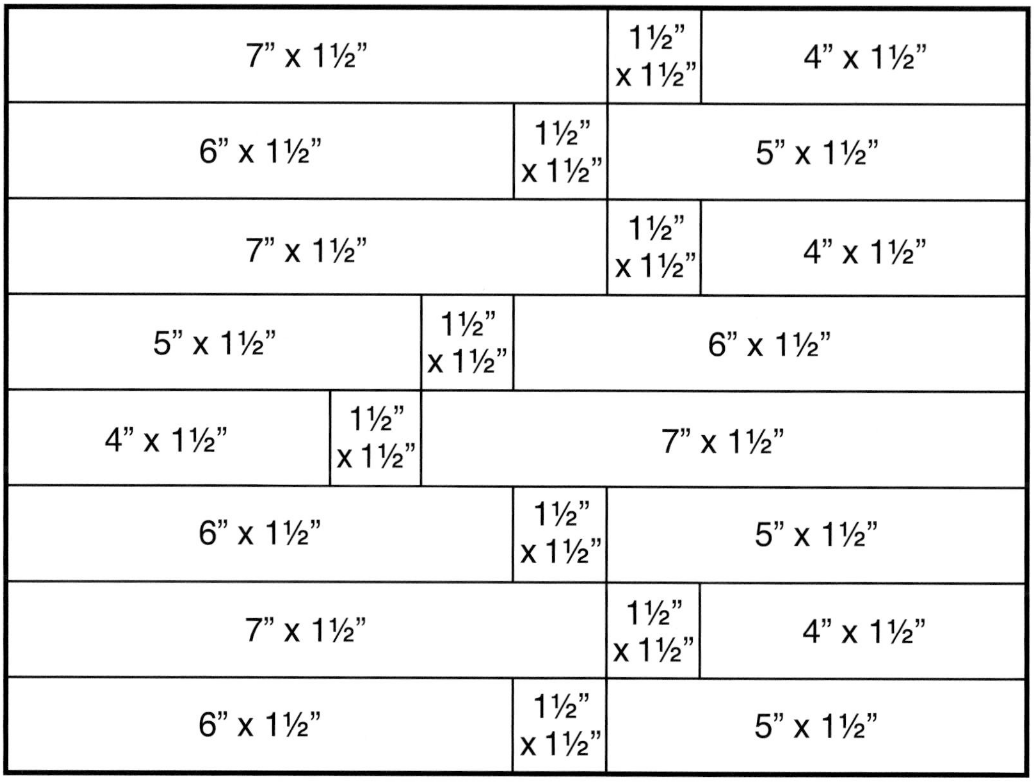

Finished block size is 11" x 8" (unfinished 11½" x 8½")

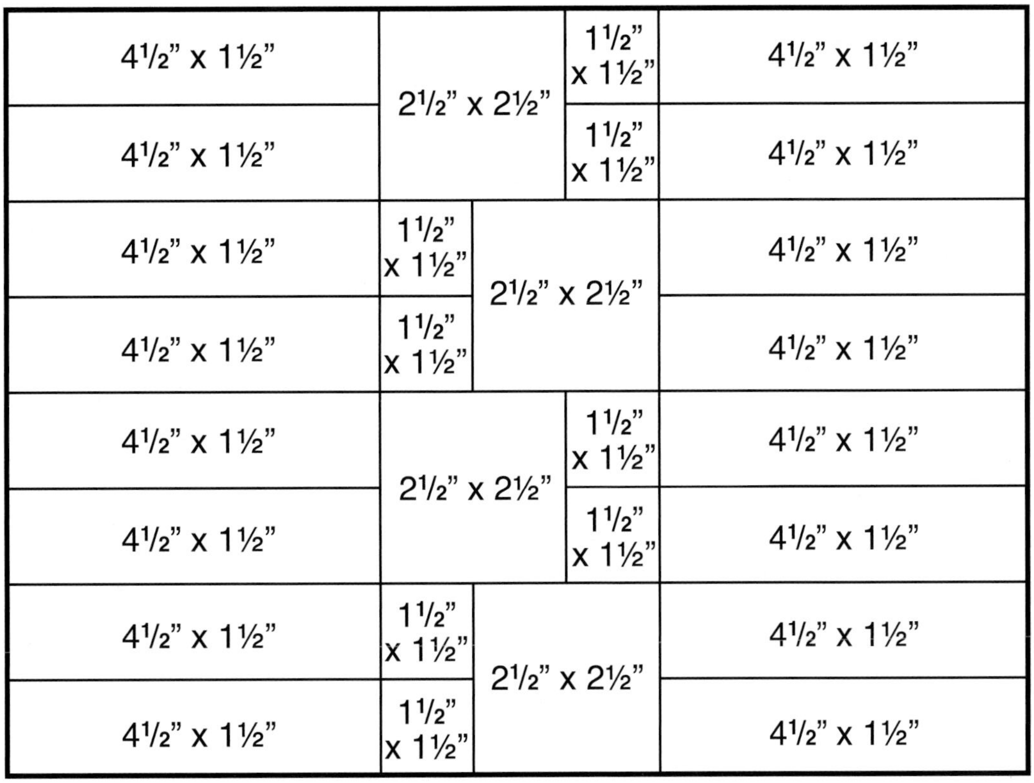

4½" x 1½"	2½" x 2½"	1½" x 1½"	4½" x 1½"
4½" x 1½"		1½" x 1½"	4½" x 1½"
4½" x 1½"	1½" x 1½"	2½" x 2½"	4½" x 1½"
4½" x 1½"	1½" x 1½"		4½" x 1½"
4½" x 1½"	2½" x 2½"	1½" x 1½"	4½" x 1½"
4½" x 1½"		1½" x 1½"	4½" x 1½"
4½" x 1½"	1½" x 1½"	2½" x 2½"	4½" x 1½"
4½" x 1½"	1½" x 1½"		4½" x 1½"

Finished block size is 11" x 8" (unfinished 11½" x 8½")

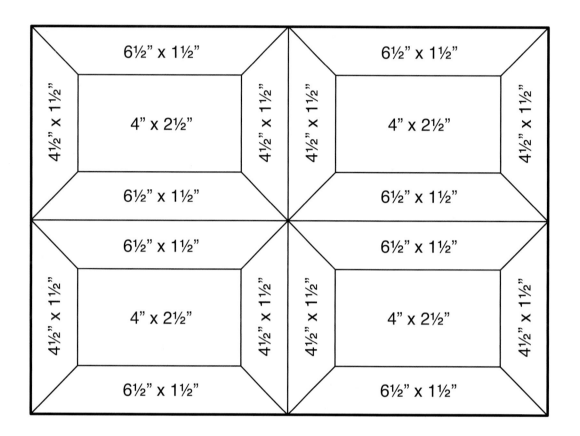

Finished block size is 11" x 8" (unfinished 11½" x 8½")

Block 7

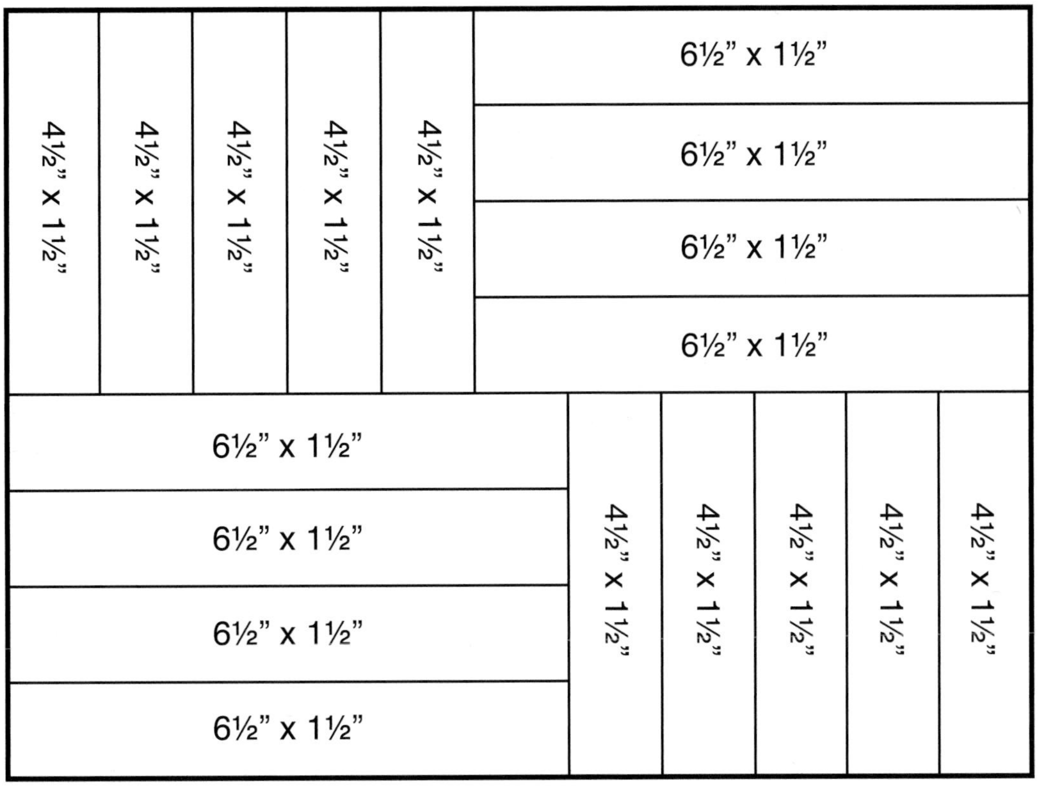
4½" x 1½"
4½" x 1½"
4½" x 1½"
4½" x 1½"
4½" x 1½"
6½" x 1½"
6½" x 1½"
6½" x 1½"
6½" x 1½"
6½" x 1½"
6½" x 1½"
6½" x 1½"
6½" x 1½"
4½" x 1½"
4½" x 1½"
4½" x 1½"
4½" x 1½"
4½" x 1½"

Finished block size is 11 " x 8" (unfinished 11½" x 8 ½")

4½" x 1½"

4½" x 1½"

4½" x 1½"

4½" x 1½"

4½" x 1½"

4½" x 1½"

4½" x 1½"

4½" x 1½"

4½" x 1½"

4½" x 1½"

4½" x 1½"

4½" x 1½"

4½" x 1½"

4½" x 1½"

4½" x 1½"

4½" x 1½"

4½" x 1½"

3½" x 1½"

3½" x 1½"

3½" x 1½"

3½" x 1½"

4½" x 1½"

4½" x 1½"

4½" x 1½"

4½" x 1½"

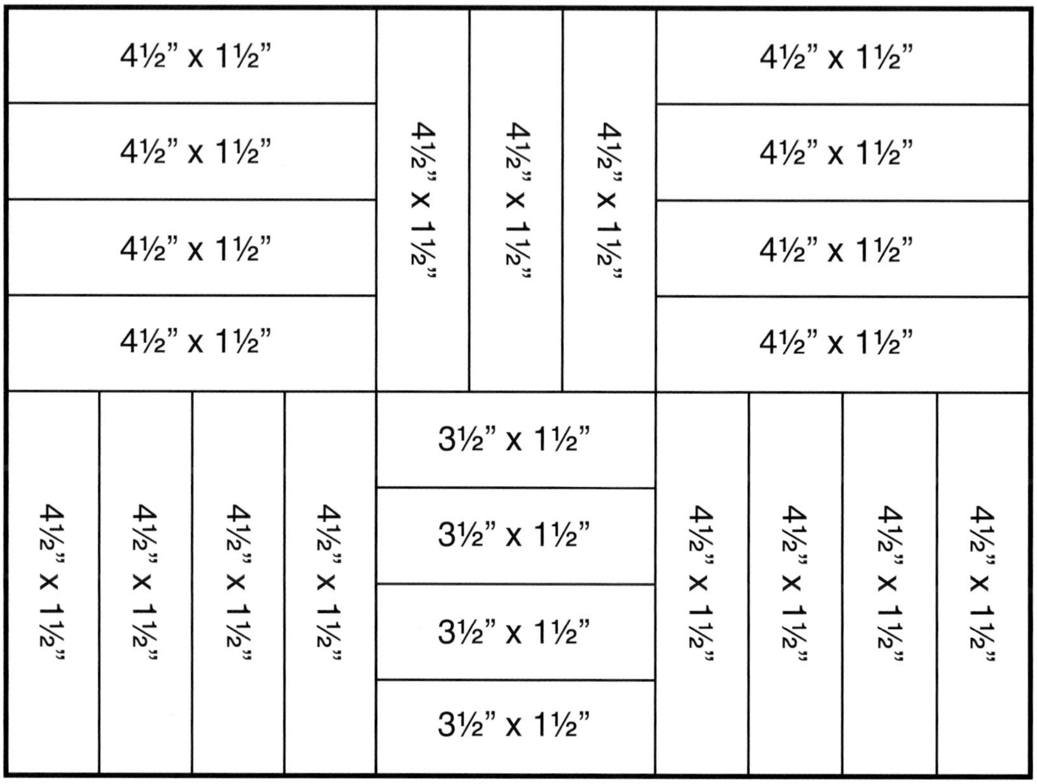

Finished block size is 11" x 8" (unfinished 11½" x 8½")

7½" x 1½"	4½" x 1½"
6½" x 1½"	5½" x 1½"
8" x 1½"	4" x 1½"
7" x 1½"	5" x 1½"
6" x 1½"	6" x 1½"
6½" x 1½"	5½" x 1½"
5½" x 1½"	6½" x 1½"
7½" x 1½"	4½" x 1½"

Finished block size is 11" x 8" (unfinished 11½" x 8½")

2½" x 2½"	2½" x 2½"	7½" x 1½"		
		7½" x 1½"		
5" x 1½"		2½" x 2½"	2½" x 2½"	3" x 1½"
5" x 1½"				3" x 1½"
3" x 1½"	2½" x 2½"	2½" x 2½"	5" x 1½"	
3" x 1½"			5" x 1½"	
7½" x 1½"			2½" x 2½"	2½" x 2½"
7½" x 1½"				

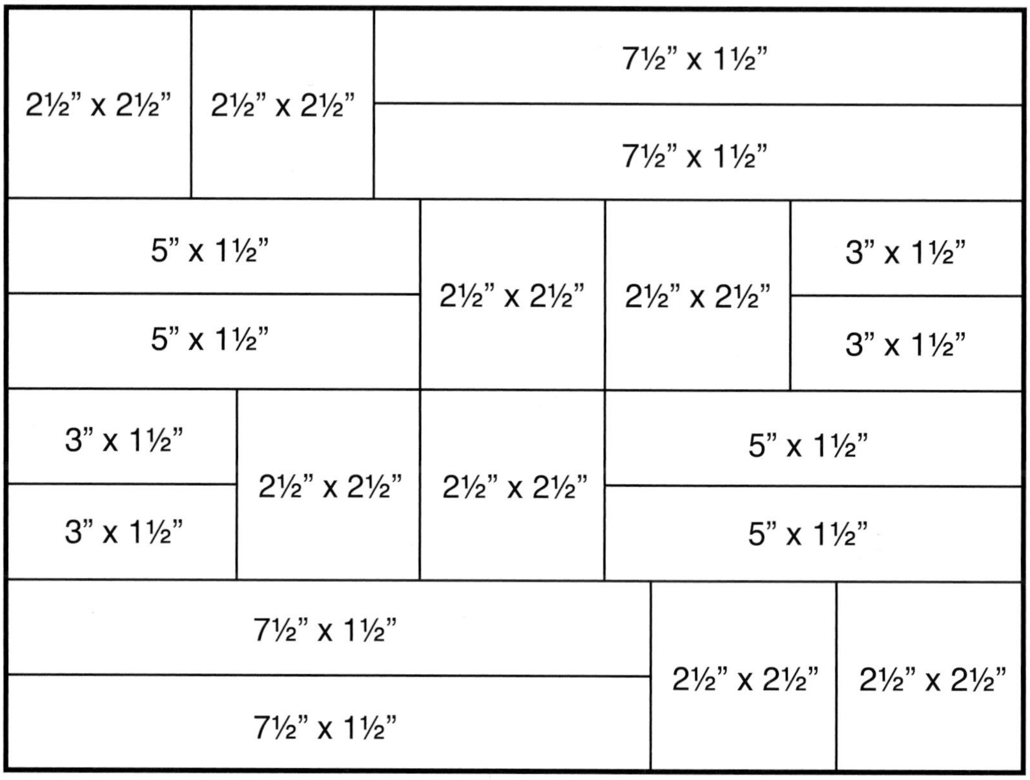

Finished block size is 11" x 8" (unfinished 11½" x 8½")

4 ½" x 1½"	3 ½" x 1½"				
4 ½" x 1½"	2 ½" x 1½"	2 ½" x 2 ½"	3 ½" x 1½"	4 ½" x 1½"	4 ½" x 1½"	4 ½" x 1½"
4 ½" x 1½"					

4 ½" x 1½"

2 ½" x 1½"

3 ½" x 1½"

4 ½" x 1½"

2 ½" x 2 ½"

3 ½" x 1½"

4 ½" x 1½"

4 ½" x 1½"

4 ½" x 1½"

4 ½" x 1½"

4 ½" x 1½"

3 ½" x 1½"

2 ½" x 2 ½"

3 ½" x 1½"

2 ½" x 1½"

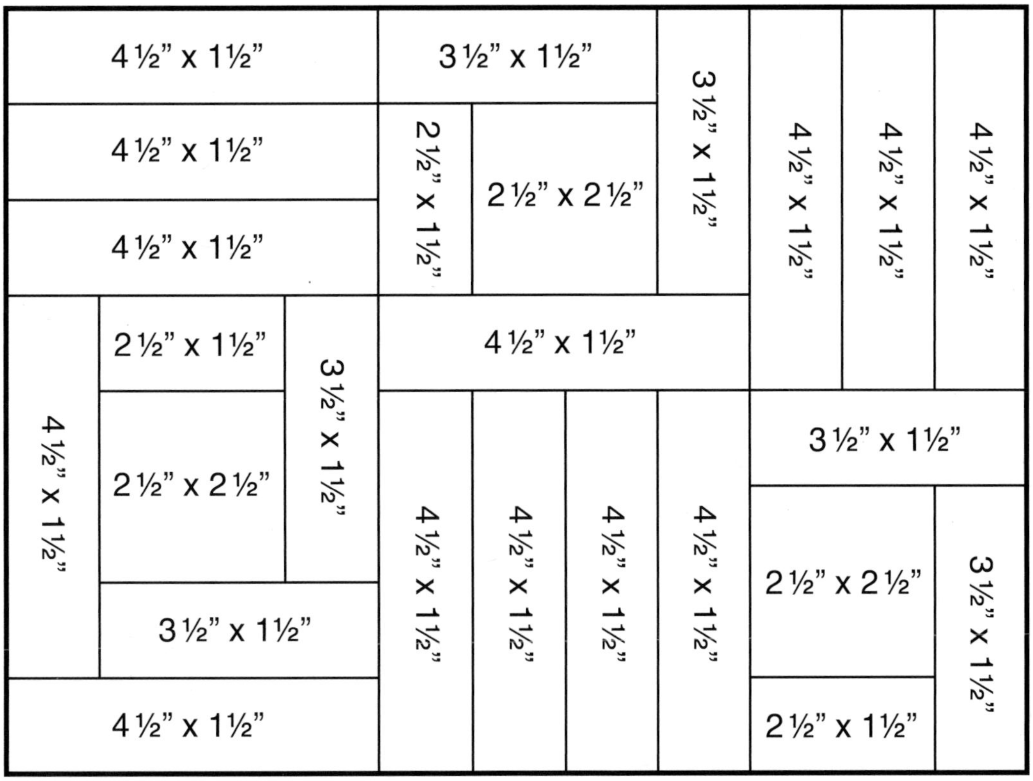

Finished block size is 11" x 8" (unfinished 11½" x 8½")

Basket A Piecing

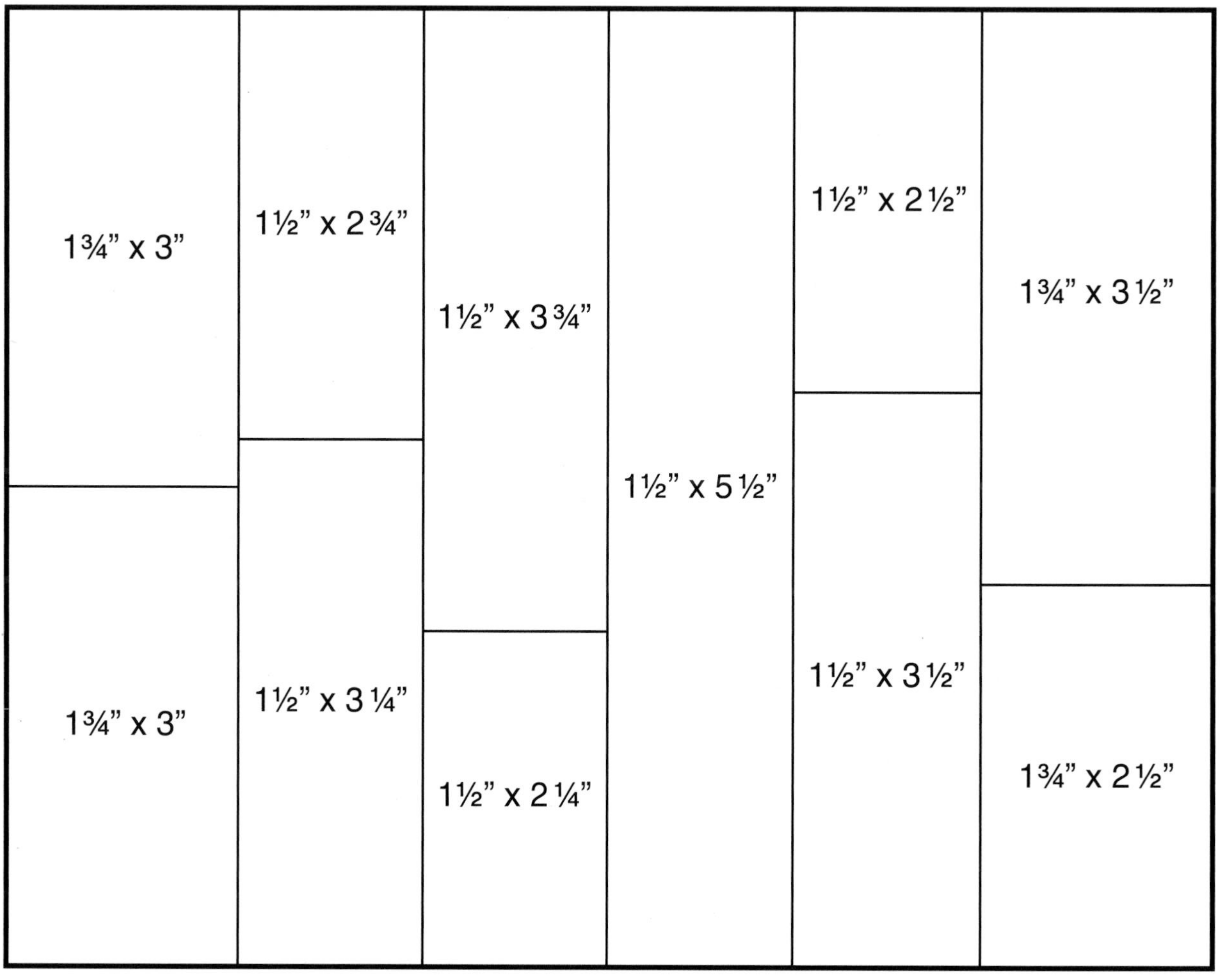
1¾" x 3"
1¾" x 3"
1½" x 2¾"
1½" x 3¼"
1½" x 3¾"
1½" x 2¼"
1½" x 5½"
1½" x 2½"
1½" x 3½"
1¾" x 3½"
1¾" x 2½"

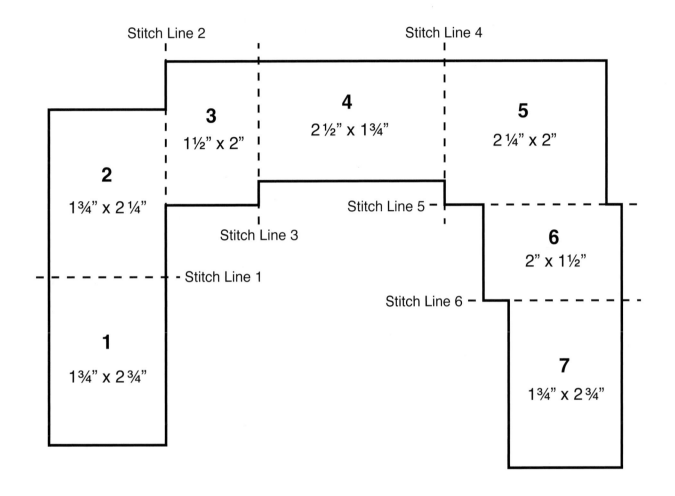

Stitch Line 2

Stitch Line 4

3

1½" x 2"

4

2½" x 1¾"

5

2¼" x 2"

2

1¾" x 2¼"

Stitch Line 5

Stitch Line 3

6

2" x 1½"

- Stitch Line 1

Stitch Line 6

1

1¾" x 2¾"

7

1¾" x 2¾"

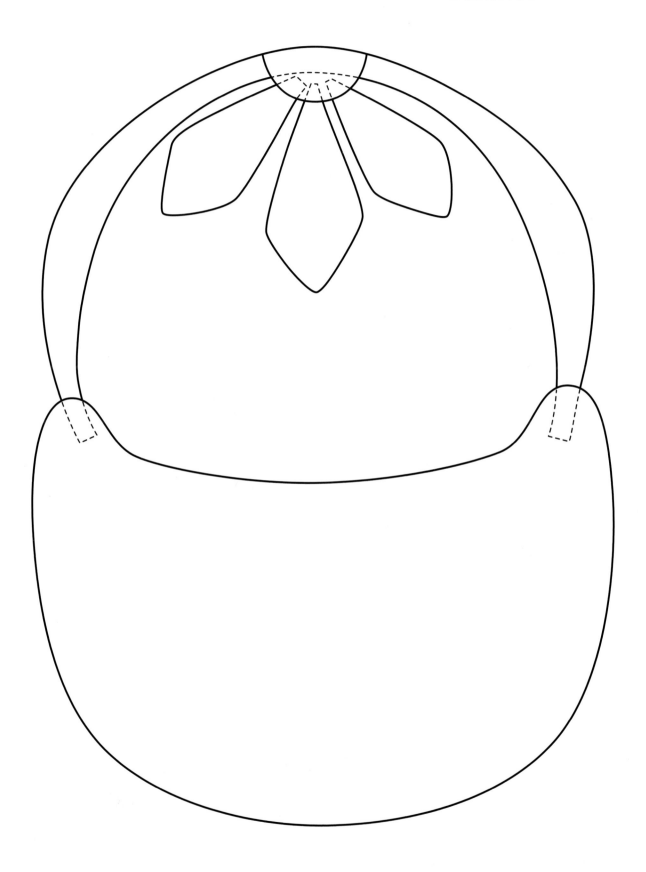

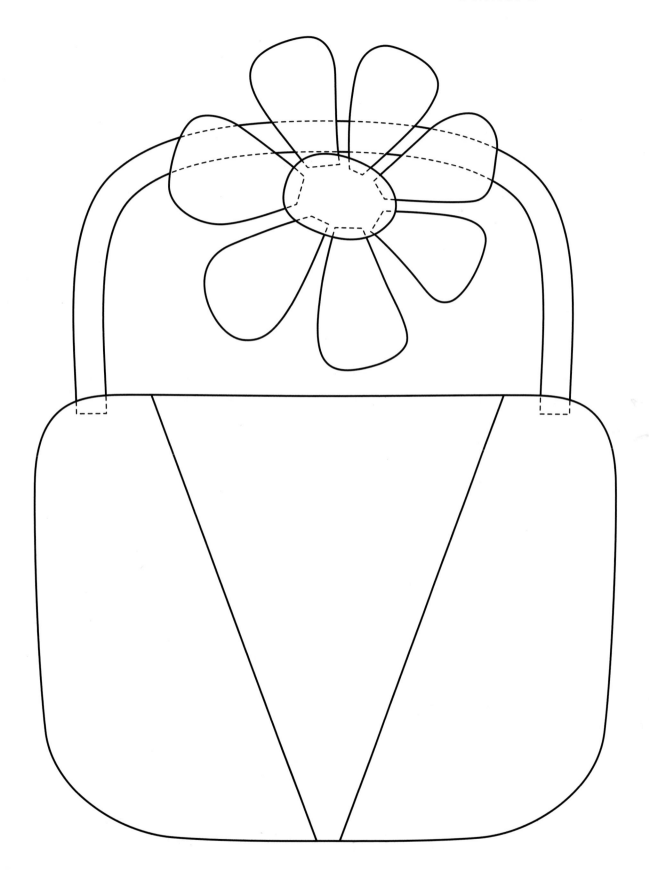

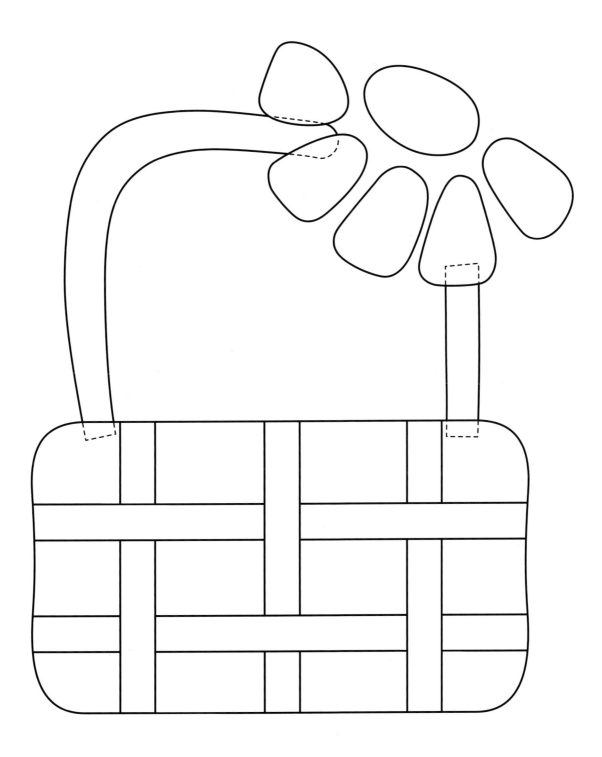

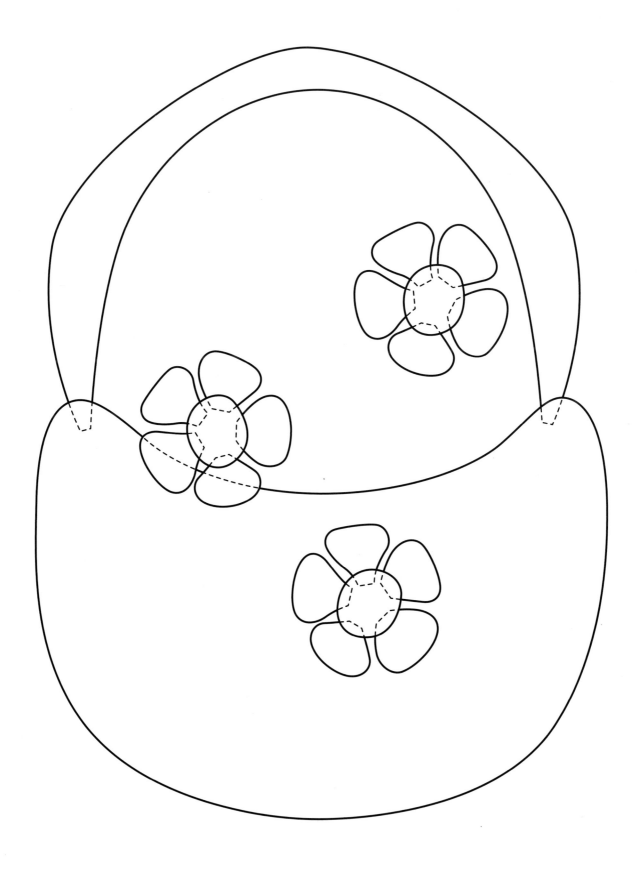

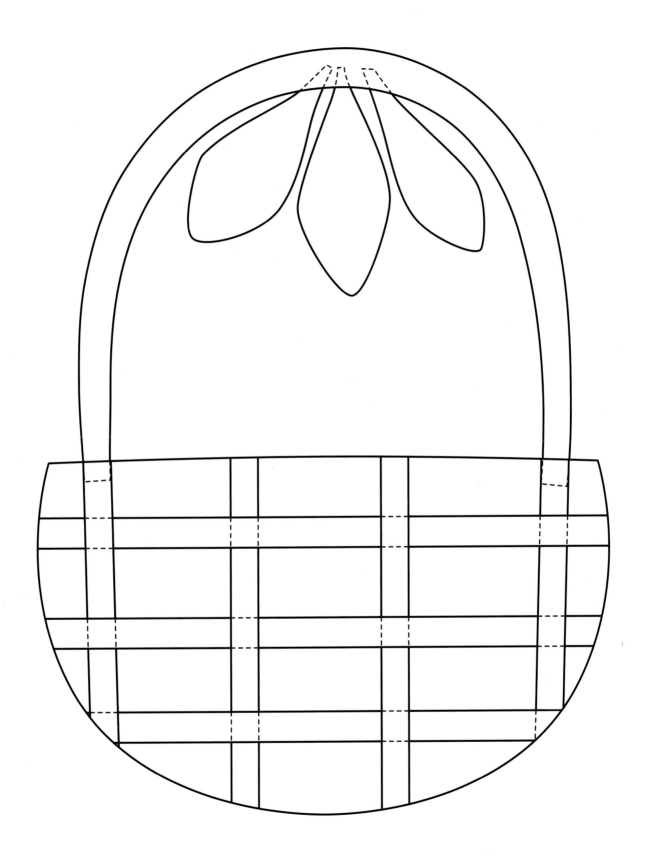

Piecing for Basket I

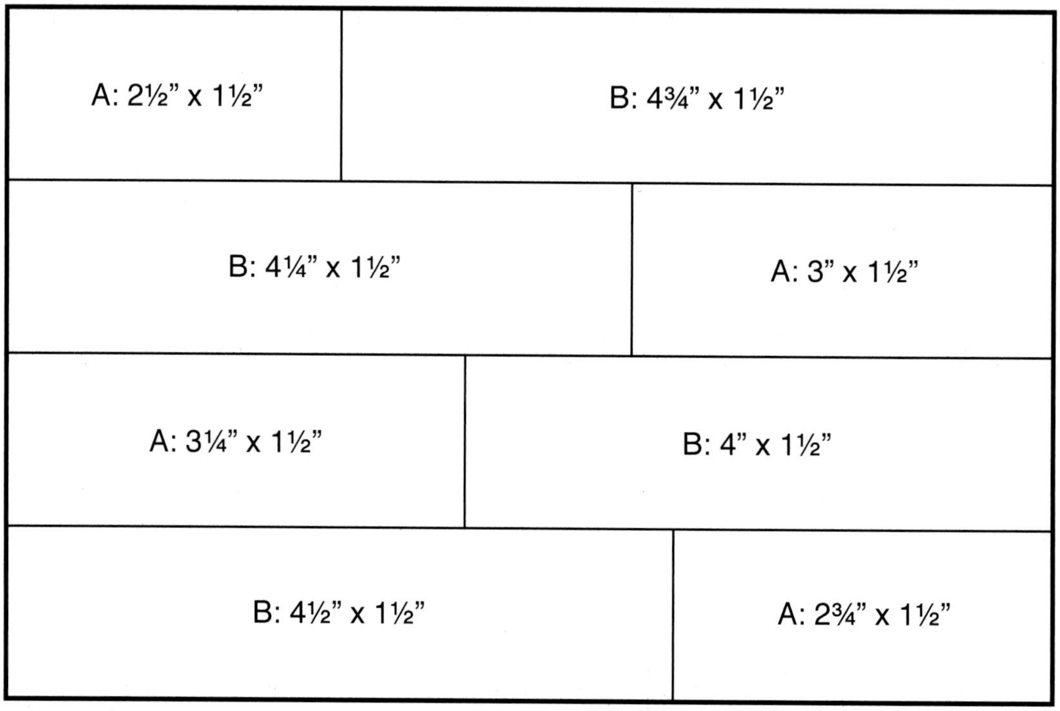
A: 2½" x 1½"
B: 4¾" x 1½"
B: 4¼" x 1½"
A: 3" x 1½"
A: 3¼" x 1½"
B: 4" x 1½"
B: 4½" x 1½"
A: 2¾" x 1½"

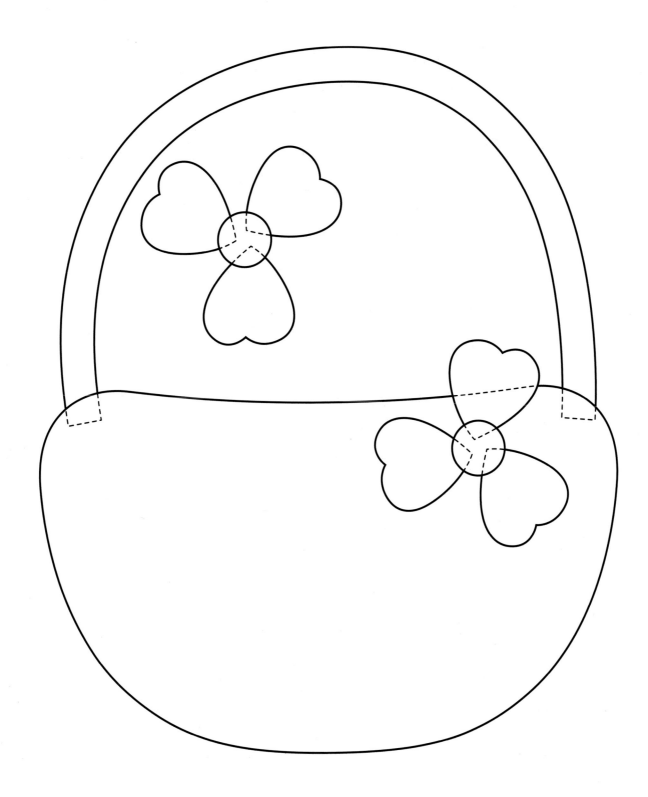

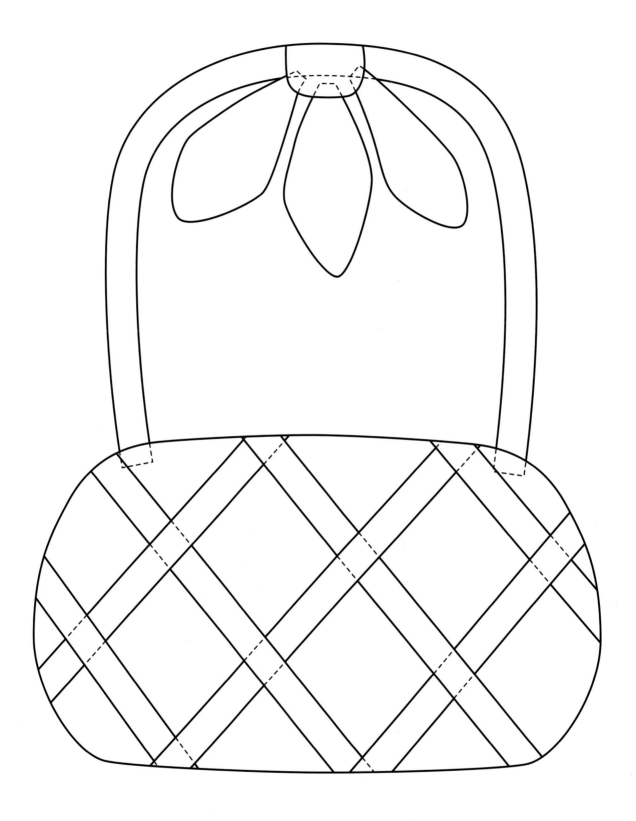

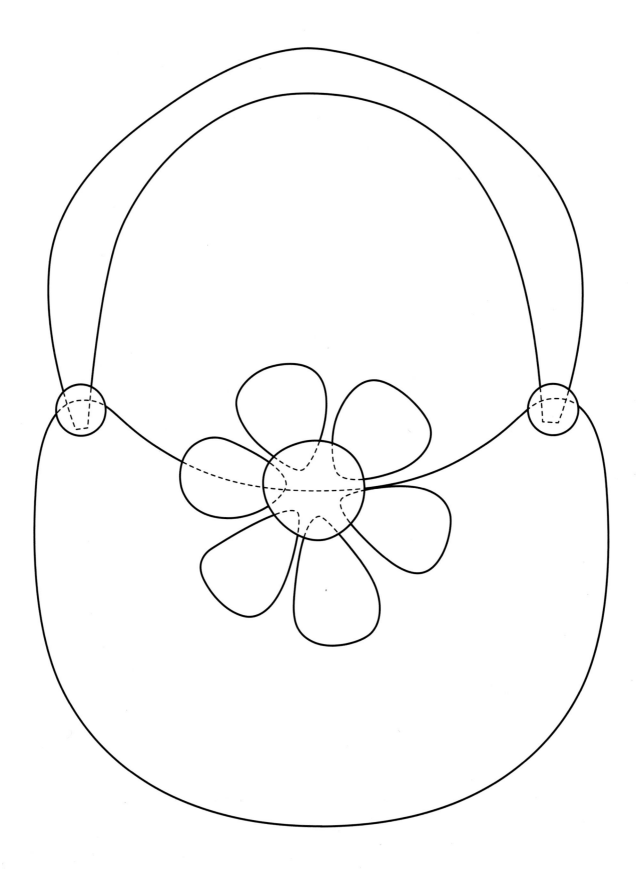

| 2½" x 10½" | 2½" x 10½" | 2½" x 10½" | 2½" x 10½" | 2½" x 10½" | 2½" x 10½" |

1 ½" x 4 ½"	2 ½" x 2 ½"	2 ½" x 2 ½"	1 ½" x 4 ½"
1 ½" x 4 ½"			1 ½" x 4 ½"
1 ½" x 4 ½"	2 ½" x 2 ½"	2 ½" x 2 ½"	1 ½" x 4 ½"
1 ½" x 4 ½"			1 ½" x 4 ½"
1 ½" x 4 ½"	2 ½" x 2 ½"	2 ½" x 2 ½"	1 ½" x 4 ½"
1 ½" x 4 ½"			1 ½" x 4 ½"
1 ½" x 4 ½"	2 ½" x 2 ½"	2 ½" x 2 ½"	1 ½" x 4 ½"
1 ½" x 4 ½"			1 ½" x 4 ½"
1 ½" x 4 ½"	2 ½" x 2 ½"	2 ½" x 2 ½"	1 ½" x 4 ½"
1 ½" x 4 ½"			1 ½" x 4 ½"

Petal Pincushion and Bag Templates

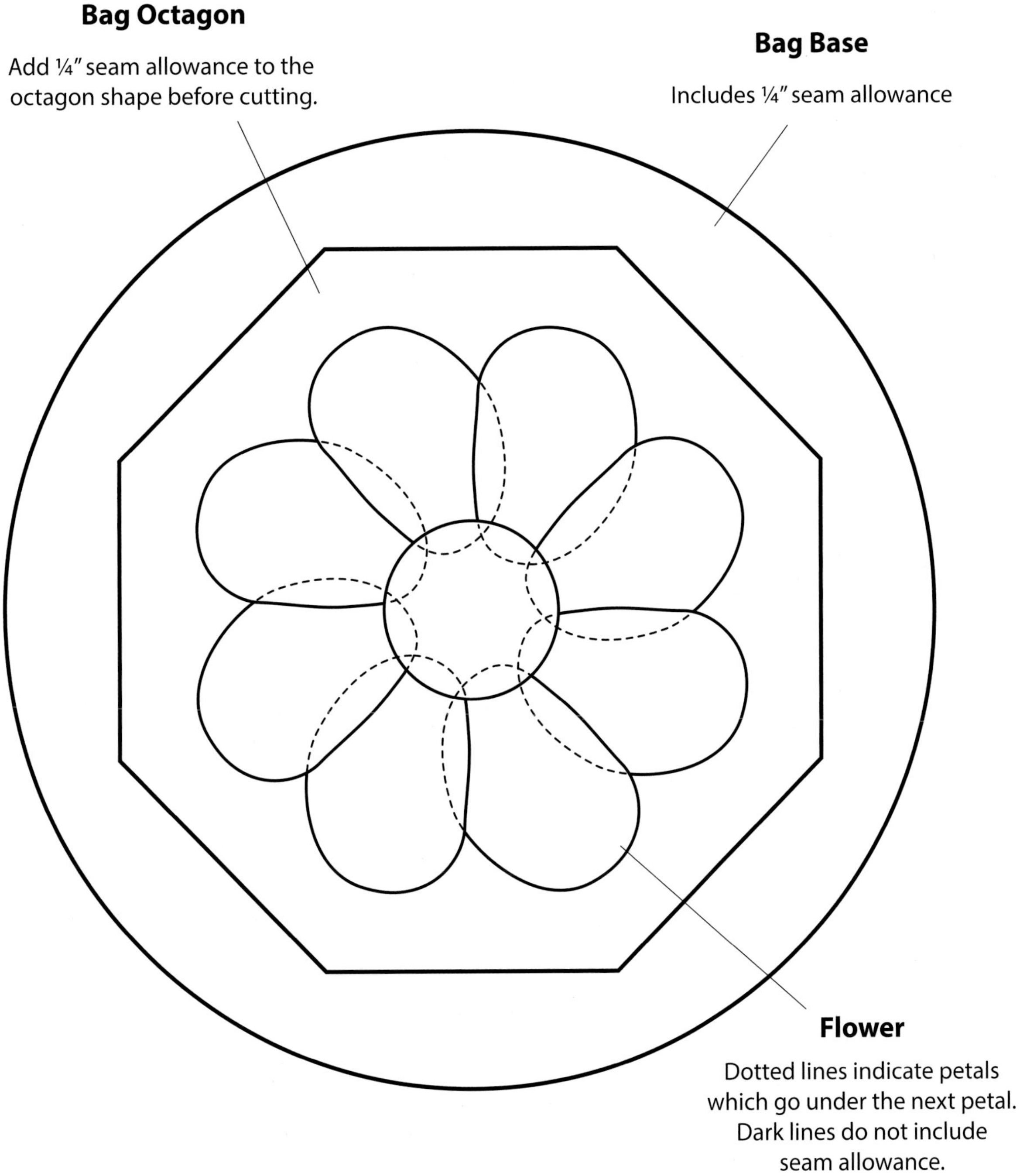

Bag Octagon

Add ¼" seam allowance to the octagon shape before cutting.

Bag Base

Includes ¼" seam allowance

Flower

Dotted lines indicate petals which go under the next petal. Dark lines do not include seam allowance.

Flower Outline for Taupe
About Town Bag

Needle Case Appliqué

Needles
and
Pins

Does not include
seam allowance.

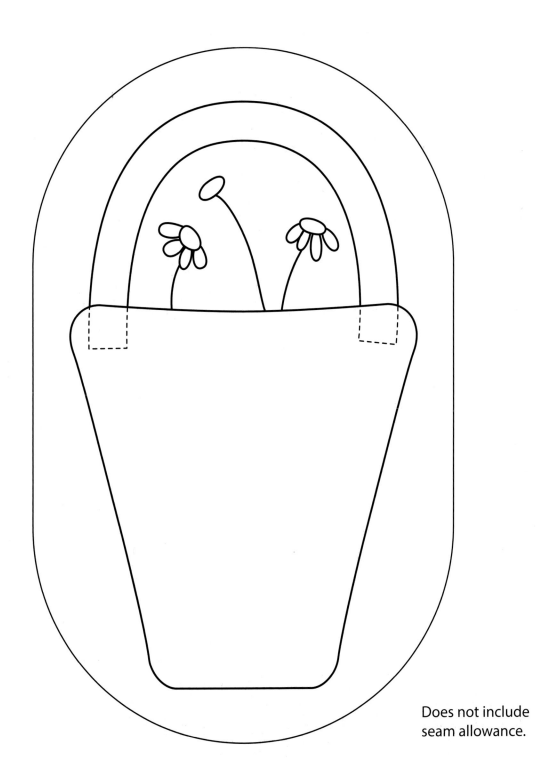

Does not include
seam allowance.

Sewing Case Appliqué
and Embroidery

Sewing
things

For pocket

Template does not include seam allowance.

92

Tumbling Block Templates

Outer template for folder back and notebook cover.
Inner template for needlecase.
Note, corners become rounded on sewing.

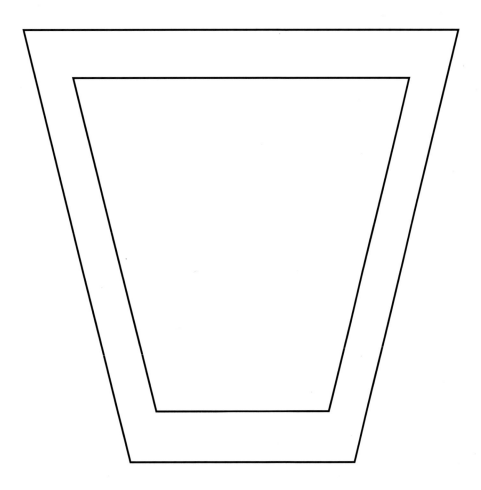

Includes seam allowance

Tumbler Pincushion Template

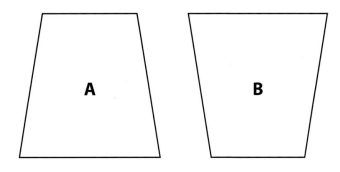

Includes seam allowance

Patterns
and
Projects